TRAVELLERS

MEXICO

By
MONA KING

Written by Mona King
Updated by Mike Gerrard

Original photography by Rick Strange, Robert Holmes
Updated photography by South American Pictures

Editing and page layout by Cambridge Publishing Management Ltd,
Unit 2, Burr Elm Court, Caldecote CB23 7NU
Series Editor: Karen Beaulah

Published by Thomas Cook Publishing
A division of Thomas Cook Tour Operations Ltd
Company Registration No. 1450464 England

PO Box 227, The Thomas Cook Business Park,
Coningsby Road, Peterborough PE3 8SB,
United Kingdom
E-mail: books@thomascook.com
www.thomascookpublishing.com
Tel: +44 (0)1733 416477

ISBN: 978-1-84157-829-3

Text © 2007 Thomas Cook Publishing
Maps © 2007 Thomas Cook Publishing
First edition © 2002 Thomas Cook Publishing
Second edition © 2005 Thomas Cook Publishing
Third edition © 2007 Thomas Cook Publishing

Project Editor: Diane Ashmore
Production/DTP Editor: Steven Collins

Although every care has been taken in compiling this publication, and the contents are believed to be correct at the time of printing, Thomas Cook Tour Operations Ltd cannot accept any responsibility for errors or omissions, however caused, or for changes in details given in the guidebook, or for the consequences of any reliance on the information provided.

The opinions and assessments expressed in this book do not necessarily represent those of Thomas Cook Tour Operations Ltd.

Printed and bound in Italy by: Printer Trento.

Front cover credits: Left © Thomas Cook; centre © Picture Contact/Alamy; right © Thomas Cook.
Back cover credits: Left © Thomas Cook; right © Thomas Cook.

Contents

KEY TO MAPS

✈ Airport   *i* Information

Ⓜ Metro station   † Church

★ Start of walk/drive   ☼ Viewpoint

3703m ▲ Mountain

Introduction

Mexico's sharp contrasts of geography, climate and culture make it a fascinating place with something for everyone. Coastal resorts offer sun and relaxation; pre-Columbian ruins beckon from deep in the jungle; colonial cities recall the grandeur of the Spanish Empire; national parks offer wildlife; and genteel spa resorts provide retreats in surroundings that attracted emperors centuries ago.

The majority of Mexicans are Spanish-speaking *mestizos*, descendants of native tribes and the Spanish. But the country also has a large indigenous population living in their ancestral lands, preserving their own language, dress, crafts and customs. Local Indian markets and fiestas make for memorable experiences.

This country of contradictions is bound to have some impact on you. Whatever your response, it won't be indifference. There is something about Mexico that sets it apart. It has a lot to do with the Mexicans themselves, who treat strangers in their midst with unusual warmth. Besides, few countries offer so much to the foreign traveller for what is still so little money. The place can work a kind of magic on you, making you want to return again and again. As the saying goes: 'Once the dust of Mexico has settled on your heart, you will find peace in no other land.'

The Temple of the Inscriptions holds the tomb of the chieftain Pakal

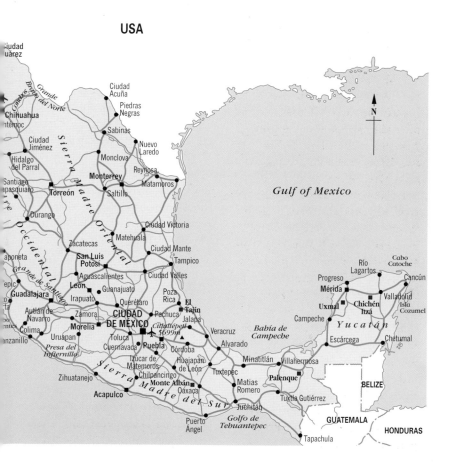

The land

Shaped rather like a horn, Mexico lies between the 14th and 32nd parallels. It shares a 3,200km (1,998-mile) border with the US to the north, and is bounded by Guatemala and Belize to the south. With an area of 1,970,000sq km (760,620sq miles), it is about a quarter of the size of the US.

Mexico is a country of dramatic contrasts, ranging from desert in the north to tropical jungles in the south; to the west lies 7,338km (4,560 miles) of Pacific coastline, while 2,805km (1,743 miles) of eastern shores border the Gulf of Mexico and the Caribbean Sea. Its wildly varying altitudes provide a richness and variety of landscapes and climates. There are three main climatic zones: the *tierras calientes* (hot lands), which go from sea level up to 800m (2,625ft); the *tierras templadas* (temperate lands), between 800m (2,625ft) and about 1,700m (5,575ft); and the *tierras frías* (cold lands), meaning elevations above this.

High country

Some 60 per cent of the land comprises mountainous terrain, and great mountain ranges dominate its landscapes. The Sierra Madre Oriental and the Sierra Madre Occidental run down the east and west of the country, respectively. These are linked by the volcanic range known as the Sistema Volcánica Transversal, which forms a natural divide between the north and south of the country. In this area are Mexico's highest peaks, and also some of its loveliest: the beautiful snow-capped volcanoes of Pico de Orizaba (5,699m/18,698ft), Popocatépetl (5,452m/17,887ft), and Iztaccíhuatl (5,286m/17,343ft). Between the two mighty mountain ranges lies the Altiplano, or High Plateau, covering the northern and central regions of Mexico. The Sierra Madre del Sur continues along the southwest coast, terminating in the green belt of Chiapas, which borders Guatemala.

Lakes and rivers

Mexico's most attractive natural lakes are to be found in the central highlands and in the southeast. Lago de Chapala, south of Guadalajara, is the largest lake, measuring 80km by 20km (50 by 12½ miles). Others of interest in neighbouring Michoacán are Lake

Pátzcuaro, south of Morelia, and Lake Cuitzeo. Lesser known is the volcanic lake of Catemaco, southeast of Veracruz. In southern Chiapas are the Lagunas de Monte Bello, a beautiful region of multicoloured lakes. The Yucatán features many lovely lagoons with crystal-clear waters.

The most famous river in Mexico is the Río Bravo (called the Río Grande in the US), which forms a large part of the border with the US as it flows into the Gulf of Mexico. The Sonora, Yaqui and Fuerte rivers irrigate the arid north and flow into the Gulf of California. The central region is served mainly by the rivers Balsa, Lerma and Moctezuma. In the southeast are the rivers Grijalva and Usumacinta (which rises in Guatemala), both of which empty their waters into the Bahía de Campeche (Bay of Campeche). A number of dams (*presas*) in various parts of the country provide irrigation and electricity.

Rainfall

The central regions of Mexico have a well-defined rainy season, roughly between late May and early October. Rainfall is minimal in northern Mexico and Baja California, while the rainforests of southeastern Mexico are subject to much more frequent rain all year round. But, as in the rest of the world, weather patterns in Mexico seem to be increasingly less predictable. In general, the best time to visit is from November to May.

The land

Much of Mexico's landscape is mountainous

Teotihuacán

The place known as Teotihuacán began as a ceremonial site and developed into a city that became one of the most important urban centres of Mesoamerica. The people of Teotihuacán were not Aztecs; historians refer to them as Teotihuacános. A political state eventually evolved, intensive agriculture was practised and commerce with other tribes flourished. At least 10,000 people are believed to have lived on this vast, 20sq km (7¾sq miles) site, as early as 2000 BC, in scattered villages.

Trade began much later, in about AD 100, when the people recognised the potential of obsidian mining from the nearby hills. As they prospered, they built the first Sun and Moon pyramids to honour the gods Quetzalcóatl and Huitzilopochtli. The primary function of these pyramids, unlike those of Egypt, was not

The Pyramid of the Sun

Carving of the head of Quetzalcóatl on his temple

funerary. In 1971, under the Pyramid of the Sun, a lava tube was discovered that had been artificially widened and ended in a chamber that was probably the most important religious site in Teotihuacán. In 2004 human remains were discovered within the Pyramid of the Sun. The hands and feet were bound, indicating that they were enemy captives who had been sacrificed.

The peak of the Teotihuacán culture was AD 300–600. It was a tightly run theocracy, in which the high priests controlled not only the religious but also the political and scientific life of the people. The place developed into a densely populated city and also exerted a far-reaching influence on other religious centres in the region.

The site is bisected by the Avenue of the Dead. On either side there appear to have been building complexes that were probably palaces. Ordinary people lived further away in denser quarters or in dwellings around courtyards.

From the 8th century there was a gradual decline, until the city was abandoned five centuries before the Spaniards arrived in Mexico.

History

50,000 BC The first people are believed to arrive in America from Asia across the Bering Strait.

10,000 BC Tepexpan Man. The earliest human remains found in Mexico.

1200–200 BC Pre-classic period. Olmec culture develops around the Gulf of Mexico region, particularly at San Lorenzo, La Venta and Tres Zapotes.

200 BC–AD 250 Shaft Tomb culture flourishes in arc-shaped area running through Jalisco, Nayarit and Colima.

AD 200–900 Classic period. Flowering of Mesoamerican art, ceramics, writing and the invention of the calendar. Outstanding are those of Teotihuacán and the Maya who develop a highly advanced culture. Other cultures flourish at Monte Albán and Mitla (Oaxaca), and El Tajín (Gulf Coast).

900–1521 Post-classic period. Decline of Mayan cities and rise of the Toltecs in Tula, who migrate to the Yucatán in the 12th century and develop a Toltec–Maya culture. Mixtecs at Mitla and Monte Albán.

1325–45 The Aztecs found the capital city of Tenochtitlán. A dominant Mexican empire grows, wielding influence and power over a wide region.

1511 Shipwrecked Spaniard Gerónimo de Aguilar is captured by Yucatán Mayas; he later becomes interpreter for Cortés.

1519 Hernán Cortés sets sail from Cuba and lands near Veracruz. He marches with about 500 men to the Aztec capital of Tenochtitlán. Emperor Moctezuma is imprisoned and killed. Bitter fighting ensues for two years.

1521 The fall of Tenochtitlán and the end of the Aztec civilisation. Completion of the Conquest of 'New Spain' and start of the colonial period. A new capital is built and called México.

1524	Twelve Franciscan friars arrive to set up missions.
1535	The first Spanish Viceroy arrives in Mexico.
1692	Insurrection in Mexico City: the Viceroy's Palace and City Hall are set ablaze by mobs.
1767	The Jesuits are expelled from Spain and its empire by order of Carlos III.
1804	All Church property is expropriated by the Crown.
1810	Father Miguel Hidalgo's famous rallying cry, El Grito de Dolores, signals the outbreak of the War of Independence against Spain.
1821	Agustín de Iturbide enters Mexico City with the Three Guarantee Army (one religion, solidarity among all social groups and an independent constitutional monarchy). The Treaty of Córdoba is signed, confirming Mexico's independence after 11 years of bitter fighting.
1822	The First Empire: General Iturbide declares himself Emperor of Mexico.
1824	The monarchy is dissolved, and a constitution adopted.
1836	Texas, New Mexico, Arizona and California declare their independence from Mexico.
1846–8	Following conflict over Texas, war breaks out between the US and Mexico. Mexico City falls to US troops. Under the Treaty of Guadalupe, Mexico recognises independence of Texas, New Mexico, Arizona and California.
1858	Benito Juárez becomes president. Reform Laws are instituted.
1862	Mexico's suspension of repayments on its external debt leads to joint intervention by Britain, France and Spain. The French army is defeated in Puebla on the 5th of May.
1863–4	The French take Mexico City and offer the Imperial Crown to the Habsburg Archduke Maximilian.

History

1864–7 The Second Empire: Maximilian reigns briefly as emperor of Mexico. Wars in Europe result in French troops withdrawing from Mexico. Maximilian is captured by Benito Pablo Juárez's troops in Querétaro, and executed on the Hill of Bells. The Republic is reinstated, and Juárez elected president.

1876 Porfirio Díaz is elected president. His long term of office is marked by foreign investment, development and growth, but also increasing discontent over land ownership and other injustices.

1910 Mexican Revolution, led by Francisco Madero, Emiliano Zapata and Pancho Villa (*see p116*). Díaz flees the country, Madero assumes presidency, but is assassinated in 1913. Bitter fighting, further assassinations and changes of presidents continue for 10 years.

1917 The new constitution comes into effect, and is still in force today.

1919 Zapata, fighter for agrarian reforms, is assassinated.

1920 The revolution officially ends.

1938 President Lázaro Cárdenas expropriates British and American oil companies and nationalises oil.

1946–52 The presidency of Miguel Alemán Valdés is a period of economic growth and tourism development.

1968 Economic growth goes hand in hand with increasing repression, both startlingly illustrated in 1968. Ten days before the Olympic Games are due to open in Mexico City, months of political unrest culminate in the Tlatelolco Massacre, when 200–300 students (some say thousands) are killed by government troops. The Mexican athlete Norma Enriqueta Basilio becomes the first woman to light the Olympic cauldron from the Olympic flame.

1976–82 Under the administration of President José López Portillo, the peso is devalued and banks are nationalised. The country plunges into economic and political crisis. Many Mexicans start emigrating, legally or illegally, to the United States, a problem which persists to this day.

1985   A major earthquake devastates Mexico City.

1986   Carlos Salinas de Gortari becomes president.

1994   The North American Free Trade Agreement (NAFTA) takes effect.

A peasant uprising breaks out in Chiapas.

Salinas is succeeded by Ernesto Zedillo as president.

The peso is suddenly devalued, a decision known as the 'December Mistake'.

The US President, Bill Clinton, grants Mexico a $50 billion loan to help stabilise the peso.

1997   PRI candidate Cuauhtémoc Cárdenas is elected mayor of Mexico City. The PRI loses its majority in Congress.

2000   Vicente Fox is elected president as PAN (Partido Acción Nacional), the major opposition party, brings to an end seven decades of PRI rule.

2003   A freedom of information law comes into force for the first time ever, allowing government records to come under public scrutiny.

2006   Felipe Calderón, the PAN candidate, is declared the winner of the presidential elections by a wafer-thin majority. The PRD candidate, Andrés Manuel López Obrador, claims that the voting was rigged and his supporters occupy parts of Mexico City. Obrador then announces an alternative government, to rule alongside the official government.

President Felipe Calderón

Spanish rule

In 1519, the Aztec empire controlled the entire Valley of Mexico, and its influence extended even further. Tenochtitlán, the Aztec capital, was a city of some 300,000 inhabitants. How could Hernán Cortés, with about 500 men and 16 horses, bring about the downfall of such an established power? A number of factors made this feat possible. Not the least of these was that Cortés burnt his ships after landing, thus ensuring that the Spaniards would conquer or die.

The Spaniards also had no idea of the numbers they were facing, not only Aztecs, but numerous other tribes over whom the Aztecs maintained dominance. As they progressed towards the capital, the Spaniards fostered alliances with some of these tribes. They were also greatly aided by two interpreters: Gerónimo de Aguilar, a shipwrecked Spaniard captured by the Mayans eight years earlier, and his mistress La Malinche, one of 20 maidens offered to Cortés in Tabasco, who was fluent in Maya and Náhuatl.

Cortés was also helped by the superstitious awe with which the Indians regarded both the Europeans and their horses. The emperor, Moctezuma, anxiously interpreted

This relief carving shows Cortés and his men with their Indian allies entering Mexico City

prophesies and portents, and the Spaniards were able to establish a relatively secure toehold on the Aztec capital.

Battles and skirmishes continued, however, and, during one of these, Moctezuma was killed. His death, on top of the Spanish edict prohibiting human sacrifice, roused the Aztecs to such an extent that Cortés was forced to retreat from Tenochtitlán. In 1521, he returned to the capital to defeat the Aztecs once and for all. He razed their temples and used the stones to build churches and homes in a new city he called México. Despite bitter resistance, the task of settling the whole country was finally completed by about 1600.

The conquistadores' declared that their purpose in conquering the land they called New Spain was to convert the natives to Christianity, but individually they were driven by the opportunity of amassing great wealth. Discovering silver, gold and other minerals, the Spaniards opened lucrative mines. They also developed agriculture along European lines and formed large feudal estates.

The religious conversions by the missionaries, however, were as important as the Spaniards' military triumph. Franciscans, Jesuits, Dominicans and Augustinians dealt with the natives directly, learned their languages, earned their trust, converted the majority, and so paved the way for the fusion of the two cultures.

Thus began 300 years of colonisation and rule by Spain. Virtually every major city in present-day Mexico was planned and developed during the 16th century, on a pattern that most cities retain till the present day. Cities in New Spain centred on a plaza around which were located the church, government buildings, and business and professional premises; eventually these plazas acquired trees, fountains and almost always a bandstand, and became the focus of the town's social activities.

By the early 19th century resentment had increased against the *gachupines*, the elite class. In 1808, responding to hundreds of real and perceived indignities, a group formed to consider breaking with Spain. A series of events led to the rallying cry for independence, Father Miguel Hidalgo's famous *grito* (cry), on 16 September 1810: 'My children . . . Will you be free? Will you make the effort to recover from the hated Spaniards the lands stolen from you 300 years ago . . . ?' After eleven years of fighting, the Mexicans won their independence.

HERNÁN CORTÉS

1485 Cortés is born in Medellín, Spain.
1504 Cortés sails to Hispaniola (now the Dominican Republic).
1511 Forms part of an expedition which conquers Cuba.
1519 Sets sail for present-day Mexico with 11 ships, 508 soldiers, about 100 sailors, some Cubans and 16 horses. Puts ashore at San Juan de Ulúa, near Veracruz. Heads for the Aztec capital of Tenochtitlán, enters and is received by Emperor Moctezuma.
1519–21 Two years of bitter fighting ensue. On 13 August, after a final battle, Tenochtitlán falls, and Cortés takes his place in history as the conqueror of Mexico.

Politics

Mexico's political system has basically followed the same line since the late 1920s. Under the constitution of 1917, the president is elected for a single six-year term and appoints his cabinet ministers. The legislative body of government is the Congress of the Union, which consists of the Chamber of Deputies and the Senate.

The political party in power for nearly 70 years, the Partido Revolucionario Institucional, or PRI (originally the Partido Nacional Revolucionario or PNR), reigned supreme until the elections of 1988, when other parties began to gain strength.

Carlos Salinas de Gortari, who was elected president by a narrow margin in 1986, introduced radical economic and political measures to address some of Mexico's structural problems. He set up an ambitious privatisation programme, and strongly promoted NAFTA (the North American Free Trade Agreement) between Mexico, the US and Canada.

Mexico seemed poised for change. But the grave problems of worsening inequalities remained. Then the country's stability was severely shaken by a series of events.

As NAFTA took effect on 1 January, 1994, an uprising of guerrillas broke out in Chiapas. Calling themselves the Zapatista National Liberation Army (EZLN), they made demands for economic change, land and autonomy. Violent clashes ensued with the Federal Army. The assassinations of Luis Donaldo Colosio, the PRI's popular presidential candidate, and another senior PRI official deeply shocked the nation. Instability resulted in the value of the peso falling by the end of the year.

When Ernesto Zedillo assumed the presidency in December 1994, he faced many problems. The devaluation of the peso caused an economic and confidence crisis, resulting in the negotiation of a financial aid package with the US and major multilateral international lending agencies.

After seven decades of PRI rule, the Mexican people voted in record numbers during the general elections of the year 2000, and Vicente Fox, who was the candidate for the opposing party, PAN (Partido Acción Nacional), won the presidency.

The country had gone through serious economic recessions in the past decades, which led to enormous

'. . . *at regular distances we continually passed over new bridges, and before us lay the great city of Mexico in all its splendour.*'

DÍAZ DEL CASTILLO

History of the Conquest of Mexico, 1568

Monument to the 1910 revolution

financial crises, and a devastating devaluation of the national currency at the start of every presidential term. Now, for the first time in its history, the transition of power took place without a devaluation of the peso or an economic crisis.

Under PAN rule Mexico slowly started to transform itself, but, as the 2006 election showed, it is still very much a divided country politically. Relations with its big neighbour to the north, the United States, remain awkward, as the US prepares to build a fence to protect its southern borders from increasing numbers of immigrants from Mexico and the rest of Central America.

Culture

Mexico has three major eras: pre-Columbian (c.1500 BC–AD 1521), colonial (1521–1821) and contemporary (from 1821 onwards). Travelling around the country is inevitably a journey through the complexities of its history and mixed cultural heritage.

Pre-Columbian cultures

Some 3,000 years ago, at the southern edge of the Gulf of Mexico, the Olmecs emerged as the first great civilisation in Mesoamerica. This mother culture flourished until about 400 BC, and its achievements influenced other civilisations (notably those of Monte Albán, the Maya and the Aztecs). Their class system, with power and knowledge concentrated in a single group, was the prototype for later societies.

Warfare was a way of life in Mesoamerica. Torture and human sacrifice were used not only in religious rituals, but also in sporting events and building dedications.

Over the centuries, other civilisations rose and fell. The artistic influence of the Teotihuacán culture covered a wide area. The Zapotecs and Mixtecs, who inhabited the valley of Oaxaca, were skilled potters and craftsmen, and covered their buildings with carvings and mosaics. The Maya achieved great sophistication in astronomy, mathematics and architecture. The last and greatest of these civilisations was that of the Mexicas, also known as Aztecs. By the time the Spaniards arrived, they were well advanced in sculpture, engineering and picture-writing. Surviving from the Maya and Náhuatl cultures are many well-preserved documents covering myths, legends, proverbs and riddles.

Colonial art

The conquest of Mexico saw the birth of a new cultural era. Art forms found expression in the context of the Christian religion; styles of architecture progressed from Baroque to Churrigueresque (an ornate extension of Baroque) and, in a minor way, Neo-Classical. An early type of decoration was called 'plateresque' (from the Spanish word for silversmith, *platero*), because of the finely carved ornamental motifs that characterised it.

Some churches, notably around Puebla, are the work of Indians, whose

Mosaic on the University Library, Mexico City

skills were recognised and encouraged by the Spaniards.

The mural movement

After Independence in 1821, the tradition of adorning religious buildings with carvings and murals was lost for nearly a century. The revolution of 1910–20 saw its revival. Painters were commissioned to execute murals on public buildings based on themes from Mexican history.

The great figures of this school were Diego Rivera, José Clemento Orozco and David Siqueiros. Rufino Tamayo, their contemporary, worked independently. Influences from the past are also clearly visible in the works of more contemporary muralists, such as Juan O'Gorman, who made hundreds of mosaics for the Library at University City in the nation's capital.

Old traditions

Native music and traditions still survive in some areas, often combined with Spanish or other influences. The fiestas, held year-round throughout Mexico, are the best example.

Many of the colourful handicrafts you can see today are produced by local artisans, using techniques that have been handed down for centuries. Each region in Mexico has its own distinctive costumes. Traditional attire is still daily wear for some indigenous peoples, such as the Tarahumaras in the northwest, and Yucatán women and various groups in Chiapas. In other places, these clothes are brought out only for fiestas and special occasions. One of the most attractive garments is the colourful *china poblana* from Puebla, considered the national costume of Mexico.

QUETZALCÓATL

The cult of this god (the plumed, or feathered, serpent) developed in Teotihuacán and continued among the Toltec, Maya and Aztecs. Mixcóatl, first leader of the Toltec people, had a son who took the name of Quetzalcóatl. He became leader of the Toltecs, and founded their new capital (present-day Tula) around AD 999.

According to one story, he threw himself on to a funeral pyre on the beach and ascended to the skies to become the morning star and ruler of time. Another says he set out to sea on a raft of snakes and vanished, while yet another relates that he reached the Yucatán, where the cult of Quetzalcóatl (or Kukulcán) was introduced by the Maya. When Quetzalcóatl set sail, he vowed to return from the east and claim his land. The year prophesied for this coincided with the arrival of Cortés and his band in 1519.

Fiestas and fairs

Every town and village in Mexico has at least one annual fiesta, in addition to nationally celebrated fiestas and public holidays, so it's quite possible you will run across one in the course of your travels. Should you wish to see a particular one, check details beforehand, as the date could suddenly change. The following is a selection of some of the best Mexico has to offer.

February/March
Mardi Gras (Carnival Week)
Late February/early March, all Mexico.
A jamboree of lively celebrations, parades with decorated floats, music, dancing and fireworks occurs just before Ash Wednesday. Massive celebrations in Veracruz and Mazatlán.

April
Semana Santa (Holy Week) Impressive Passion Play in Ixtapalapa, just outside Mexico City. Beautiful candlelit processions in Taxco. (Palm Sunday to Easter Sunday)
Feria de San Marcos (St Mark's Fair)
Lively fair in Aguascalientes with bullfights, cockfights, *charreadas*, *mariachis*, dancing. (Around 25 April to 5 May)

May/June
Corpus Cristi Of special interest is the old Totonac ceremony of the Voladores (Flying Men) of Papantla, which takes place in Papantla, Veracruz.

Día de San Antonio (St Anthony's Day) Entertaining in San Miguel de Allende, where Los Locos (The Crazy Ones) parade through town in masks and strange costumes. (13 June)

July
La Guelaguetza Week-long festivities take their name from the Zapotec word meaning 'participate by cooperation'. It is one of the most beautiful fiestas in Mexico, with the cultural heritage of all seven Indian regions of Oaxaca on full display; parades, dances, food, music, and more. An unforgettable feast for the senses.

September
Día de la Independencia (Independence Day) Mexico's most important annual date, commemorating the outbreak of the War of Independence against Spain. Grand celebrations in Mexico City. Its highlight is the *Grito*, given by the President from the National Palace on

the 15th. The following day is marked by a military parade, including elegant *charros* (cowboys) on horseback. (15–16 September)

October
Festival Internacional Cervantino (International Cervantes Festival) This cultural festival in Guanajuato, named after the author of *Don Quixote,* has become a big international event. Over a two-week period there are concerts, plays, opera and other cultural events, with participants from many nations.
Fiestas de Octubre A month of continuous celebrations in Guaddajara, with concerts, art exhibitions and numerous sporting and cultural events, crowned by glorious fireworks.

November
Día de los Muertos (Day of the Dead)

Especially unique on the tiny island of Janitzio in Lake Pátzcuaro. At midnight the villagers go to the cemetery with torches and candles, carrying flowers and food offerings for their departed ones. The whole island comes alive with thousands of flickering lights as the natives take part in the vigil. (1–2 November)

December
Día de Nuestra Señora de Guadalupe (Festival of Our Lady of Guadalupe) Commemoration Day of the Patroness of Mexico. Endless processions of pilgrims arrive in Mexico City from all over to pay homage at the Virgin's shrine, the Basilica of Guadalupe, one of the most revered in the country. Regional dancers in resplendent costumes perform native dances in front of the Basilica. (12 December)

In Champotón, Campeche, a religious procession follows behind a banner portraying Our Lady of Guadalupe

Impressions

Mexico is like a kaleidoscope, with many sides to its nature. No two people see it alike. There are plenty of misconceptions about the country, but, if you go with an open mind and a positive attitude, you will be well rewarded. A sense of adventure helps too! Don't expect anything to be like it is 'back home' – it won't be. Better to expect the unexpected. As the song claims, 'Como México no hay dos', 'There is only one Mexico!'

Culture shock

Arrival at Mexico City airport is, in itself, quite an experience. A great barrage of faces hits you as you emerge. Mexican families and their children come here *en masse* to await relatives and friends. Porters try to grab your bags and there is a general air of frenzied activity.

It takes a little time for the traveller to adjust, even physically, to the city. Its high altitude (over 2,000m/6,560ft above sea level) and chronic air pollution must be taken into account (many visitors experience sore or dry throats). Take things at a slower pace than usual, and try not to cram too much into the first couple of days. The city is always bustling with life. The continuous movement and noise may well seem rather overwhelming until you start to get into the rhythm of things.

Etiquette and customs

Mexicans are known for their carefree attitude and capacity to enjoy life, and also their great sense of humour. They are by nature warm and friendly, and more than willing to be helpful. But you must be prepared for the fact that, while a question will always get a reply of some sort, it may not be the right one at all, as the emphasis is often on pleasing you rather than on accuracy!

People here much appreciate the little courtesies in life, so that *gracias* (thank you) and *de nada* (not at all) feature

THOMAS COOK'S MEXICO

Cook's began to advertise Mexico as a tourist destination in 1885, following the opening of the railway between the US and Mexico City, and the resumption of diplomatic relations between Mexico and Britain. The first Cook's agency in Mexico City opened the same year at Calle San Francisco, providing a foreign exchange service and hotel accommodation advice. Mexico soon became a popular winter resort, and a Cook's brochure for 1891–2 promised visitors 'every attraction possessed by the famous resorts of the Old World together with many charming features peculiar to itself'.

ETHNIC GROUPS

Over time, Mexican society was divided into four main ethnic categories: the *peninsulares* or *gachupines* (Spaniards born in Spain); *criollos* (of Spanish blood but born in Mexico); *mestizos* (mixed Spanish and Indian, by far the largest ethnic group today); and the *indígenas* (Indians).

regularly in the course of conversation. They also believe in proper greetings with handshakes or an *abrazo* (a hug) between friends.

Like many, the Mexicans' sense of national pride can express itself too strongly at times and, while they themselves can be critical of their country's shortcomings, they may not take kindly to criticism from others.

The people of Mexico appear shy and modest, but this does not mean that they are unfriendly. They are a dignified people, whose unshakeable pride in their heritage demands respect.

Family life

Life in Mexico revolves around the family, which takes priority above everything else. There are strong feelings of love and loyalty within families, who will go to extraordinary lengths to help one another. Both old and young have a very special place in the heart of all Mexicans.

Although Mexicans generally entertain out, they are a naturally hospitable people. The expression *'Usted tiene su casa'* ('This is your home') is a commonly used courtesy. But it can lead to a genuine invitation to come home and meet the family – and, when it does, you know you have really been taken to their hearts.

The stunning façade of the Metropolitan Cathedral

Impressions

Linguistic nuances

You can get by in good restaurants, hotels, some shops in Mexico City, and in tourist centres without any knowledge of Spanish. English is not normally spoken in more modest restaurants. Some effort on your part is always appreciated, however, even if it only amounts to such basics as *buenos días* (good morning), *buenas noches* (goodnight) and, most important, *gracias* (thank you).

Naturally, you stand to gain if you speak some Spanish. Apart from helping in sorting out problems, you can pick up many useful bits of information from taxi drivers, barmen or other local people. Travelling independently off the beaten track becomes difficult if you don't speak the language. In addition to Spanish, a number of different languages and dialects are spoken by the various Indian groups in their regions. These are mostly away from the usual tourist areas, with the exception of Mérida, and generally in the Yucatán. If you

Detail of the monument to Benito Juárez in Alameda Park, Mexico City

listen carefully, you will hear the local people conversing very softly in Mayan.

Machismo

No account of Mexico would be complete without reference to the famous *machismo*, with which it is often associated. The Mexican *macho* tends to be portrayed as a dashing *charro* (rodeo rider) astride his horse, or swaggering into a bar with a stetson and a low-slung belt. *Machismo* is a sort of demonstration of maleness and of outdoing other men. It manifests itself in many ways. Young men show daring by driving fast and recklessly, or by diving feats off the cliffs in Acapulco.

Most towns and villages have men-only *cantinas* and snooker bars. This is not out of disrespect for women – rather to the contrary. Being on the rough side, these places are felt to be inappropriate for women. Mexicans respect their women and feel protective towards them, with chivalry still very much alive here. A man will open a door for a woman, walk on the streetside with her, and very rarely permit her to pay for a meal or a drink. When his own woman is concerned, he can be very possessive. Should she be subject to any provocative attention from another male, the *machismo* can really show!

Women

Women are gradually becoming more emancipated and career-minded. Using their femininity, however, can

Women are increasingly being given better educational opportunities

sometimes achieve more than trying to compete with men on their own level. A woman on her own in a bar, restaurant or public place is likely to attract attention. She would be well advised to avoid provocative clothing or behaviour, and to deal with any unwelcome advances by a shake of the head or a firm 'No'!

The mañana syndrome

The *mañana* mentality of leaving things until the following day, or some unspecified time, is a broadly Latin one, but it has certainly found a home in Mexico. Not for nothing are Mexicans fond of the saying: 'Never do today what you can put off until tomorrow, and never do tomorrow what you can put off forever.' It must be said, however, that the Mexican has imagination and a feeling for improvisation. When all else seems

hopeless, they have a way of getting everything done – just in time.

Touts

As in many tourist countries, you may well be pestered by people who want to sell you something you don't want. In Mexico City, the travel touts work the tourist areas around hotels. You will come across them in the Zona Rosa offering to guide you to the pyramids, markets, around the city, whatever. It is wise to ignore them, as they are unlikely to be registered guides, and may not offer what they claim. It's best to book a tour through your hotel or a reputable travel agency. Unless you want to pay over the odds, avoid taxi touts, very visible in Mexico City, at the airport or cruising the streets in large flashy cars. Never hail a taxi on the street – assaults still occur. Instead get one at a fixed *sitio* site, or phone for a radio taxi.

Though rugged and wild, the Copper Canyon is home to a gentle people, the Tarahumara Indians

Where to go

If travelling independently to Mexico for the first time, you will have the task of choosing which destinations to include and, more difficult, which to leave out. Mexico offers such a diversity of attractions that it is not easy to decide. Whatever your interests, try not to cram in too much. Distances are greater than you think. The strain of travel and the climatic and altitude changes can take their toll. Besides, there is always something unexpected to see around the next corner. Allow a little extra time in each place, just in case. Overall, two or three weeks at least are suggested for touring, with a few days in Mexico City to start off. There are many possibilities, depending on your interests.

Ancient cultures

The majority of Mexico's major archaeological sites are in the southeast. A classic tour, best done by air, includes Oaxaca, for the nearby Zapotec and Mixtec ruins of Monte Albán and Mitla; Villahermosa, as a base from which to visit the spectacular jungle ruins of Palenque; and Mérida, from which you can visit the famous Mayan cities of Uxmal and Chichén Itzá. In addition, there are numerous smaller sites dotted about the region, some of which are not easily accessible.

Colonial cities of Central Mexico

A delightful overland tour takes you along the Colonial Route, which includes the towns of Querétaro, San Miguel de Allende, Guanajuato and

Morelia, noted for their attractive architecture and historical interest in connection with the War of Independence from Spain.

The Route of the Volcanoes

A trip by road east to Veracruz via Puebla and Orizaba passes through dramatic changes of scenery, from the high altitude of Mexico City down to the steamy Gulf region. The route offers magnificent views of Mexico's famous snow-capped volcanoes, Popocatépetl, Iztaccíhuatl, Orizaba and La Malinche (*see p137*). Avoid the rainy summer months, when the volcanoes can be obscured by clouds.

Beaches

The shores of Mexico offer tremendous choice. Along the Pacific coastline are numerous resorts, ranging from Acapulco and Puerto Vallarta, to Ixtapa, and the more rustic Zihuatanejo, and resort complexes such as Las Hadas and the Bel-Air Costa Careyes. Further south, the Huatulco development contrasts with the small resorts of Puerto Angel and Puerto Escondido. The Caribbean boasts the popular resort of Cancún and the islands of Cozumel and Isla Mujeres, along with other developments down the coast.

Deserts and canyons of the north

Mexico's northern expanses include ranching areas, deserts and cacti, and the Copper Canyon (Barranca del Cobre), homeland of the proudly

traditional Tarahumara Indians. This is one of the most scenic and interesting areas in the country, though somewhat off the beaten track. A trip on the Copper Canyon railway is most rewarding (*see pp140–41*).

Baja California

If you are looking for something different, this is it. This long, narrow peninsula features vineyards and olive groves, deserts and mountains, wild rocks and seas, and clear blue skies. It is thinly populated, and offers excellent watersports and great outdoor life, plus a reliably pleasant climate.

Artistry of another age adorns the entrance to this church in Atlixco, Morelos

What to wear

Pack light and focus on casual, comfortable clothes. However, you must take into account climate and the nature of the area. Mexico City requires more formal clothes. Men may need a tie and jacket for the more sophisticated restaurants, where trouser outfits for women are quite acceptable. Between December and February, women may need a light-weight coat for cool evenings. Otherwise a jacket should suffice. Cotton will feel better than synthetic materials.

When touring around, make sure you have comfortable shoes for exploring cobblestone streets and ruins. Take something warm for cold evenings at higher altitudes. Women do not have to cover their heads when entering a church. Be appropriately covered as occasion demands, for example, in hotel restaurants. Topless sunbathing

Hats and canopies keep off the heat

and nude swimming are not acceptable in Mexico. Take something to cover your head against the tropical sun, and a raincoat or foldaway umbrella during the rainy months.

When to go

November to May is the best time to visit Mexico. You can expect a good climate, warm waters for swimming, and greener landscapes immediately after the summer rains. The peak

Fruit and nuts for sale at Playa del Carmen

tourist season is around mid-December to mid-April, when hotel rates can be considerably higher in the popular coastal resorts. The summer months are hot and rainy, while September's weather can be unsettling, with storms and the occasional hurricane, particularly in the Gulf of Mexico and Caribbean, and the southern part of Baja California.

Dry fields with corn stooks under Iztaccíhuatl

Mexico City

Mexico City (Ciudad de México), which includes the Distrito Federal, the nation's capital, has grown into a sprawling metropolis with an estimated population of 20 million (out of the country's total of 108 million). It claims to be the world's most populous city and, at 2,240m (7,349ft) above sea level, is also one of the highest. You will get an idea of its size if you fly over it and see the vast conurbation, ringed by mountains, spreading across the Valley of Mexico. Arrival at night is an impressive experience, as the whole valley looks like a carpet of glittering lights.

The city was built in 1521 by the Spaniards on the ruins of the Aztec capital of Tenochtitlán. Today, it is a blend of modern skyscrapers, wide boulevards and narrow streets, churches and colonial buildings. Referred to by the Mexicans simply as México, or the Distrito Federal (DF), it is the hub of the country. The altitude can cause shortness of breath and tiredness, but should not overly affect anyone enjoying normal health. Smog is an unfortunate problem here, but there are many beautiful days when you can enjoy the city under clear, blue skies.

The feel of the city

Exploring Mexico City requires stamina and patience. Wide boulevards, large intersections, heavy traffic and high, uneven pavements can be discouraging. But it is always interesting and full of surprises. The streets are bursting with colour, noise and activity. Mexico City boasts the longest street in the world,

Avenida Insurjentes, which spans the entire city and extends beyond. The best

areas to explore on foot are the historic centre around the Zócalo, the Zona Rosa, along the Paseo de la Reforma, and Chapultepec Park. In some districts street names follow particular themes, such as famous cities (in the Zona Rosa), rivers, or great writers and philosophers – a useful clue to locating the neighbourhood.

Tourist information office: Pres Mazaryk 172, Polanco. Tel: (55) 3002 6300, ext 111, or freephone from inside Mexico (01 800 987 8224).
www.mexicocity.com.mx
Open: Mon–Fri 9am–6pm & Sat 9am–2pm.

High-rise Mexico City

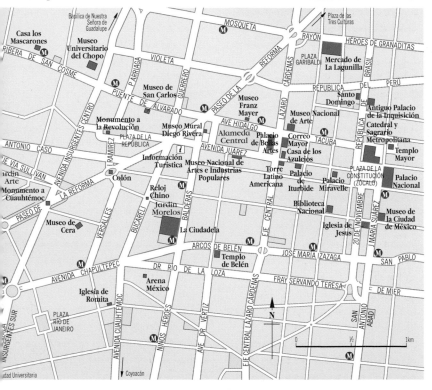

Alameda Central

This is Mexico City's central park, dating back to the end of the 16th century, adorned by graceful bronze Italian statues, paths, fountains and many varieties of trees. In front stands an impressive marble monument to Benito Juárez. On Sundays, the place teems with families out for a stroll. *Between Avenida Juárez & Avenida Hidalgo. Open: daily. Free admission. Metro: Bellas Artes or Hidalgo.*

Basílica de Nuestra Señora de Guadalupe

The Basilica of Our Lady of Guadalupe is regarded as the holiest place in Mexico (*see p48*). According to legend, it was here, in December 1531, that an Indian boy, Juan Diego, saw a vision of the Virgin Mary, who asked that a church be built in her honour. When advised of this, the local bishop asked for proof. The Virgin appeared again, asking the boy to gather some roses from nearby. This he did, and when he opened his cloak to show them to the bishop, the beautiful image of the dark-skinned Virgin was imprinted on it. A church was built on the site and consecrated as a shrine, with the Virgin of Guadalupe declared the Patron Saint of Mexico.

The imposing old basilica, which is sinking into the subsoil, has been replaced by a contemporary-style church built alongside it, designed by Pedro Ramírez Vázquez. The shrine is the object of year-round pilgrimages. A moving stairway takes you slowly past the Virgin's image on Juan Diego's cloak. *10km (6¼ miles) north of downtown. Tel: (55) 5577 6088. Open: daily 6am– 9pm. Free admission. Metro: Basilica.*

Bosque de Chapultepec

Chapultepec Park covers an area of over 810ha (2,000 acres) of parkland, with woods, fields and lakes. Used by the Aztecs, it is one of the oldest natural parks in North America. It features magnificent *ahuehuetes* (giant cypress trees), some of which are centuries old. Mexicans bring their children here on Sundays to enjoy the amusement park, the zoo and boating on the lake. Also located in the park are the Museum of Anthropology (*see pp34–5*), Chapultepec Castle (*see below*) and other museums (*see pp36–7*). *West of Mexico City. Open: daily. Metro: Chapultepec.*

Castillo de Chapultepec

Chapultepec Castle stands high up on a hill, overlooking the Park and Mexico City, with a magnificent view of the Paseo de la Reforma. First built as a castle in the 18th century, it later became a military academy and, in 1847, was the scene of a battle with US troops, during which six young cadets died defending the school. An impressive monument in front of the castle, *Los Niños Héroes* (The Young Heroes), commemorates the event.

The Habsburg Emperor Maximilian and his wife Carlotta resided here during his short reign (1864–7). It now

functions as the **National Museum of History**, with interesting relics of the life and times of Maximilian, in addition to varied displays of art and everyday objects depicting Mexican life from the Conquest to 1917.
Section 1 of Chapultepec Park. Tel: (55) 5241 3100. Open: Tue–Sun 9am–4.30pm. Admission charge.

Catedral Metropolitana

The Metropolitan Cathedral – the largest in Latin America – stands on the Zócalo, the capital's main square. It is an imposing edifice, constructed on the site of an earlier church built in 1532 by the Spaniards following the Conquest, which was later demolished in favour of the present cathedral. It wasn't finished until 1813, and hence presents various styles of architecture. Adjoining it is the Sagrario (Sacrarium), built in the mid-1700s in rich Baroque style.

North side of the Zócalo. Open: daily 8am–7pm. Free admission.

Ciudad Universitaria

University City, located south of the centre in the Pedregal District, is the campus of the *Universidad Nacional Autónoma de México* (National Autonomous University of Mexico – UNAM), where over 300,000 students are registered. The original university was founded in 1553, to be replaced in time by the current institution.

The present campus, built in the 1950s, is noted for its striking modern architecture and bold murals. Some of the buildings considered outstanding for their design and murals are the mosaic-covered Central Library (a masterpiece by Juan O'Gorman), the School of Medicine, the Rector's Office and the Auditorium of the Science Faculty.

Mexico City

Chapultepec Castle, now a museum, proudly surveys its parkland setting

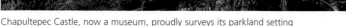

Museo Nacional de Antropología

The National Museum of Anthropology is a must-see for any visitor to Mexico City. Its unique collection of pre-Columbian art treasures, magnificently presented, places it among the world's finest museums of this kind. Opened in 1964, it was designed by renowned Mexican architect Pedro Ramírez Vázquez, and centres around a courtyard which features a single pillar supporting a huge umbrella-like concrete roof. A dramatic waterfall drops in a translucent sheet, while a huge monolithic sculpture, representing Tláloc, the god of rain, stands surrounded by water at the entrance.

The museum has three floors. On the lower ground level is the Orientation Room, where you can see models and films on Mesoamerican culture. On the upper ground floor, the Ethnography Section has a number of halls showing the style of the various Indian groups living in Mexico today. The ground floor forms the major part of the museum. Exhibition halls around the patio are devoted to the fascinating pre-Hispanic period, from earliest settlements to the blossoming of advanced civilisations. An anti-clockwise walk around takes you in and out of the various halls, with restful pauses.

Hall 1 offers an Introduction to Anthropology, with exhibits on the evolution of man. This leads to Halls 2 and 3, named Mesoamerica and Origins. Halls 4 and 5 display artefacts from the Pre-Classic Period and Teotihuacán civilisations. The Toltec Hall (No 6) includes an impressive Atlantean warrior figure from Tula, stelae (carved stone slabs or pillars) and sculptures. Outside, at the rear of the hall, is part of a temple from Tula, decorated and coloured.

Taking centre stage at the far end of the complex is Hall 7, the Mexica Hall. This is one of the most exciting areas, dealing with the Aztec, or Mexica, culture. Facing you, high up on a white marble slab, is the famous Sun Stone (or Aztec Calendar, as it is often called), depicting the face of the Sun God, Tonatiuh, surrounded by hieroglyphs of days and months interspersed with solar rays. It is, undoubtedly, a highlight of the museum, imbuing the hall with a sense of solemnity and ancient magic. Also prominently displayed are important sculptures recovered from the Templo Mayor excavations near the Zócalo. Other impressive exhibits in the hall are the model (and painting above it) of the Aztec capital of Tenochtitlán, and the reproduction of Emperor Moctezuma's plumes.

Continuing around the block, you will come to the Oaxaca Hall (No 8), which focuses on the Zapotec and Mixtec cultures, with figurines, urns and stelae. This leads to the Gulf of Mexico Hall (No 9), where you are confronted by a giant Olmec monolithic head, its negroid features pitted with tiny holes, found in San Lorenzo, Veracruz. The hall covers the period from 1200–600 BC, and contains many intriguing sculptures, including some curious Huastecan figures. The Maya Hall (No 10) is of great interest, featuring large masks found in the state of Campeche, stone carvings from Chichén Itzá, figurines from Jaina and copies of the famous Bonampak frescoes. The remaining two halls deal with the cultures of the North and the West.

Northern section of Chapultepec Park, on Paseo de la Reforma y Gandhi.
Tel: (55) 5512 3224.
www.mna.inah.gob.mx.
Open: Tue–Sun 9am–7pm.
Admission charge (Sun free till 5pm).
Cameras without flash are permitted.
Guides speaking other languages can be hired on request.

Museo Nacional de Antropología

Fascinating exhibits in ideal surroundings: the Aztec's ancient capital, Tenochtitlán

MUSEUMS

In addition to the famous Museum of Anthropology, the city has a number of museums devoted to history, art and other subjects. Unless stated otherwise, they are open daily except on Mondays.

Museo de Anahuacalli

The House of Anahuac, designed by Diego Rivera, has a collection of pre-Columbian art together with sketches by the artist.
Calle del Museo 150, Coyoacán.
Tel: (55) 5617 4310. Open: Tue–Sun 10am–6pm. Admission charge.

Museo de Arte Moderno

The Museum of Modern Art houses works by notable 19th- and 20th-century Mexican artists, and also holds temporary exhibitions.
Paseo de la Reforma y Gandhi.
Tel: (55) 5221 8331. Open: Tue–Sun 10am–6pm. Admission charge.

Museo de la Ciudad de México

Museum of the city's history, housed in an attractive former mansion.
Pino Suárez 30, Zócalo area.
Tel: (55) 5542 0083. Open: Tue–Sun 10am–6pm. Admission charge.

Museo Franz Mayer

Franz Mayer's collection of European, Asiatic and American artefacts.
Avenida Hidalgo 45, Zócalo area.
Tel: (55) 5518 2266.
Open: Tue, Thur–Sun 10am–5pm, Wed 10am–7pm. Admission charge.

Museo Frida Kahlo

Works by Frida Kahlo, her husband Diego Rivera and other Mexican artists.
Londres 247, Coyoacán.
Tel: (55) 5554 5999.
Open: Tue–Sun 10am–6pm.
Admission charge.

Museo Mural Diego Rivera

This museum was built specially to house the famous Diego Rivera mural (*Dream of a Sunday Afternoon in Alameda Central*) that was moved from the Del Prado Hotel after the devastating 1985 earthquake.
Balderas and Colón, Plaza Solidaridad.
Tel: (55) 5512 0754.
Open: Tue–Sun 10am–6pm.
Free admission.

Museo Nacional de Antropología

See pp34–5.

Museo Nacional de Historia

See Castillo de Chapultepec, *p32.*

Museo Rufino Tamayo

This museum houses the art collection of Rufino Tamayo and includes paintings by Mexican and international artists.
Paseo de la Reforma y Gandhi.
Tel: (55) 5286 6519.
www.museotamayo.org. Open: Tue–Sun 10am–6pm. Admission charge.

Palacio de Bellas Artes

The opulent, white marble Palace of Fine Arts was built between 1905 and 1934. Home of the national opera and symphony orchestra, it is also famous for its twice-weekly performances of the brilliant Mexican National Ballet Folklórico. A striking feature is the glass curtain, made by Tiffany's of New York, depicting the volcanoes Popocatépetl and Iztaccíhuatl.

Avenida Juárez.
Tel: (55) 5512 2593.
Open: Tue–Sun 10am–6pm.
Admission charge.

Palacio Nacional

Standing atop the old Aztec ruins, the building has seen several changes. From 1698 to Independence in 1821, it was the home of the Spanish viceroys. After that it housed the offices of the president of Mexico. The bell which hangs over the central porch is said to be the one rung by Father Miguel Hidalgo, the parish priest of Dolores (Guanajuato), when he rallied the populace in 1810 to take up the struggle against the Spaniards. Inside, adorning the walls over the central staircase, are magnificent Diego Rivera murals depicting the struggle of Mexicans over the centuries.

Eastern side of the Zócalo.
Tel: (55) 9158 1259.
Open: daily 10am–5pm.

Exquisite detailing above the entrance to the Palace of Fine Arts

The broad and leafy Reforma is a window on the world, with its never-ceasing bustle

Paseo de la Reforma

This is Mexico City's most famous boulevard. Extending 15km (9¹/₂ miles) from Tlatelolco in the northeast to Lomas in the west, it was built at the behest of Emperor Maximilian to link Chapultepec Castle with the National Palace on the Zócalo. Known originally as Calzada del Emperador (The Emperor's Way), it was later named Paseo de la Reforma after the Reform Laws of President Benito Juárez. From the hilltop castle there is a fine view of Reforma.

The avenue's main section, which runs from Avenida Juárez to Chapultepec Park, is attractively lined with palm trees and a variety of foliage, with several traffic lanes on the side of central pedestrian strips. At intervals are large roundabouts (*glorietas*), along with a number of monuments honouring heroes or important historical events. Notable sculptures are those of Cuauhtémoc, the last Aztec ruler, and the Columbus Monument. Most famous, and a landmark of Mexico City, is the Independence Monument, known simply as El Angel after the gilded angel that proudly crowns its imposing column.

Plaza Garibaldi

A visit to this ever-popular spot will give you a real flavour of the Mexicans' natural capacity for good, rousing fun. Numerous *mariachi* bands, dressed in their smart *charro* outfits, congregate in this square every evening and play requests for payment. With different groups playing simultaneously, the enjoyable cacophony creates an incredible ambience! *Cantinas,* restaurants and nightspots around the square all add to the lively scene. *About 10 minutes north of the Palace of Fine Arts, east of Calle Lázaro Cárdenas.*

Plaza de las Tres Culturas
See p48.

Torre Latinoamericana
The impressive 43-storey Latin-American Tower, the second-highest building in Mexico City, offers panoramic views of the city and the Valley of Mexico. Two lifts take you up to a splendid observation deck on the 42nd floor. On a clear day there is a good view of Popocatépetl and Iztaccíhuatl volcanoes.

Mexico City's grand Zócalo is the focus of much activity and entertainment

Calle Lázaro Cárdenas. Tel: (55) 5518 7423. Open: daily 9am–10pm. Admission charge to observation tower.

Zócalo
This is the main square of Mexico City and the heart of the old city. Officially named Plaza de la Constitución (Constitution Square), it is known as the Zócalo, which means 'pedestal' and refers to the base of a monument planned but never built. Most main squares in Mexico are known as *zócalos.* This vast area once boasted gardens and a bandstand. In the 1900s, however, it was all filled with concrete, and nowadays is adorned only with a large Mexican flag. The Zócalo is nevertheless most impressive, bordered by superb buildings, and full of animated activity day and night, with traditional native dances and other forms of entertainment.
Metro: Zócalo.

Zona Rosa
The 'Pink Zone' – a name whose origin is obscure – is a compact area that runs south of Reforma to Avenida Chapultepec, bounded by Insurgentes to the east and Lieja to the west. The Zona Rosa has lost some of its trendiness to other areas, such as Polanco, but it still offers a lively concentration of galleries, elegant shops, bars and restaurants, vendors and music-makers. Pedestrian streets are lined with cafés so you can sit outside and watch the world go by.

Walk: Mexico City's historic centre

This walk takes you down to the Zócalo, heart of old Mexico City, and is signposted as Centro Histórico (Historic Centre). Sunday is a good day, when traffic is minimal.

Allow 2 to 3 hours.

Start at the intersection of Paseo de la Reforma and Avenida Juárez, and walk down Avenida Juárez.

1 Avenida Juárez

As you walk down this wide boulevard you will pass, on your left, the attractive Alameda Central Park (*see p32*), a focal point of the city, fronted by a semicircular monument to President Benito Juárez. A little further on is the handsome white marble Palacio de

Bellas Artes (*see p36*), work of the Italian architect Adamo Boari, which is renowned as a venue for the spectacular Mexican National Ballet Folklórico. *Cross over Avenida Lázaro Cárdenas and then continue walking down Calle Francisco 1 Madero.*

2 Calle Francisco 1 Madero

This is an old street, and one of the most interesting in Mexico. Formerly known for its silversmiths, it still has

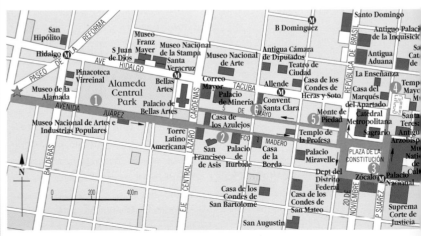

many shops selling gold and silver jewellery. Immediately on your right you will notice the Latin-American Tower (*see p39*). Over to your left is the Casa de los Azulejos (House of Tiles). Originally built as a grand town house, it is now a Sanborns restaurant and gift shop. Opposite is the 16th-century Templo de San Francisco de Asis (Church of St Francis of Assisi). Next to that is the Palacio de Iturbide. Formerly the palace of Agustín de Iturbide during his brief spell as Mexico's first emperor (1821–3), this is now a branch of Banamex Bank, with art exhibitions held in the atrium. On the corner of the Zócalo is the Hotel Majestic, with views of the grand square from its terrace. *Enter the Zócalo.*

3 The Zócalo

Officially called the Plaza de la Constitución (Constitution Square), it is usually referred to as the Zócalo – the hub of Mexico City, a grandiose square full of life (*see p39*). Turn right and into Calle 16 de Septiembre to take a look at the unusual interior of the Howard Johnson Gran Hotel. Returning to the Zócalo, you will see facing you the National Palace (*see p37*), housing various government departments. Inside, over the staircase, are the famous Diego Rivera murals depicting the history of Mexico. To the left is the Metropolitan Cathedral with the adjoining Sagrario (*see p33*). *Walk behind the cathedral to the excavations of the Templo Mayor.*

4 Templo Mayor

The Aztec remains of this 'Great Temple' were discovered quite by chance only in 1978 when workmen were laying cables for the metro. Excavations over the ensuing years revealed hundreds of sculptures, including some large pieces of great significance. The museum displays the artefacts from the dig, and portrays the past splendour of this ancient Aztec ceremonial centre of Tenochtitlán.
Tel: (55) 5542 4943. Walk back along the other side of the cathedral, cross the road and enter the Monte de Piedad.

5 Monte de Piedad

Literally meaning Mountain of Piety, this is Mexico City's National Pawnshop – a fascinating place. Dating back to 1777, it was built on the site of a former Aztec palace as a charitable organisation to help the needy. As you pass through a long arcade, you will see everything imaginable on sale, ranging from antiques and jewellery to household goods and electronic equipment. *Walk straight through. You will come out into Calle Cinco de Mayo.*

6 Calle Cinco de Mayo

Virtually the whole street is dedicated to books. Readers of Spanish can find all sorts of fascinating volumes here, and booksellers very helpful.

24-hour tourist information tel: Infotur: (55) 5250 8555.

Mexico City environs

ARCHAEOLOGICAL SITES

A number of pre-Columbian sites can be visited on day trips from Mexico City. Most are free on Sundays and public holidays. Unless stated otherwise, they are open daily, except Monday.

Cacaxtla-Xochitécatl

This ancient ceremonial site has excited attention since the discovery of highly coloured Mayan-style murals. The ruins date from around AD 200–1300. Overlooking Cacaxtla, the small ceremonial centre of Xochitécatl features four structures from the Classic period, and a stunning view of the volcanoes.
About 96km (60 miles) east of Mexico City. Tel: (246) 416 0000. Open: Tue–Sun 10am–5pm. Cacaxtla murals: 10am–1pm. Admission charge.

Calixtlahuaca

The main feature of this site is the circular temple of Quetzalcóatl, dedicated to the wind god Ehecatl. Various parts of the structure point to several cultures.
8km (5 miles) north of Toluca. Open: 10am–5pm.

Cuicuilco

One of the earliest known structures in Mexico. The area was embedded in lava after a violent volcanic eruption, and uncovered only in the 1920s.
Insurgentes Sur, 3km (1³/4 miles) west of Tlalpan. Tel: (55) 5606 9758. Open: 9am–5pm.

Malinalco

An Aztec ceremonial centre of dramatic structures hewn from stone, surrounded by forests and rock formations.
12km (7¹/2 miles) east of Tenancingo, on Mex 55. Open: Tue–Sun 9am–6pm.

Teotenango

A large site dating back to around the 7th century AD, it is thought to have been an important ceremonial centre.
25km (15¹/2 miles) north of Tenancingo, on Mex 55. Open: Tue–Sun 9am–5pm.

Tula

The remains of Tollan, former capital of the Toltec people, with Atlantean warrior figures that once supported the roof of a temple. Tollan was founded in AD 968, but abandoned in 1168 after being sacked by the Chichimecs.
85km (53 miles) north of Mexico City. Open: Tue–Sun 10am–5pm. Admission charge.

Xochicalco

Evidence links these hilltop ruins with various cultures.
36km (22¹/2 miles) southwest of Cuernavaca. Open: 9am–6pm. Admission charge.

OTHER ATTRACTIONS
Desierto de los Leones

A large parkland of coniferous forests with marked trails and the ruins of a 17th-century Carmelite monastery.

20km (12¹/₂ miles) west of Mexico City. Park open: daily. Free admission. Monastery open: Tue–Sun 10am–5pm. Admission charge.

Lagunas de Zempoala

Seven lagoons set in a national park. 62km (38¹/₂ miles) southwest of Mexico City. Open: daily. Free admission.

Tepotzotián

The façade of the Convent Church of San Francisco Javier is one of Mexico's finest examples of the Churrigueresque.

Magnificent interior. 42km (26 miles) north of Mexico City, on Mex 57. Open: Mon–Fri 9am–7pm, Sat–Sun 7am–7pm.

Tepozteco

Náhuatl, the ancient tongue of the Aztecs, is still spoken here, and certain Aztec traditions are still preserved. On the square stands a 16th-century convent. A climb of 30 minutes takes you to the Pyramid of Tepozteco. 25km (15¹/₂ miles) northeast of Cuernavaca. Tel: (739) 395 0255. Open: daily 9am–5.30pm.

Mexico City environs

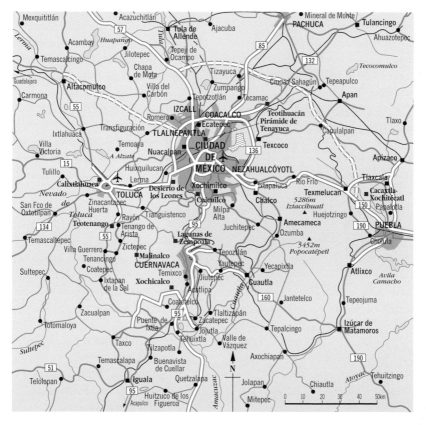

Tour: Floating Gardens of Xochimilco

This tour visits attractions south of the capital, including the University, the Olympic Stadium, the Pedregal and San Angel districts, and a boat trip on the Floating Gardens of Xochimilco.

Allow a full day, as Xochimilco alone requires approximately 3 hours to do justice to it.

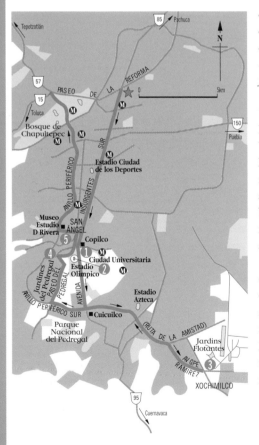

Start at the intersection of Paseo de la Reforma and Insurgentes Sur, and proceed south. Take a look at the colourful, exuberant flower market on your left.

1 Ciudad Universitaria

Founded in the 1950s, University City (*see p33*) has a large campus and some 300,000 registered students. It is worth stopping to take a look at the bold architecture and the use of murals and frescoes taken from ancient designs. Don't miss the 10-storey mosaic-decorated Central Library by Juan O'Gorman, the Rector's Office, and the former Faculty of Science and the Faculty of Medicine, which are both noted for their thought-provoking murals.

Tel: (55) 5665 0709. Cross over the road to take a look at the Olympic Stadium.

2 Estadio Olímpico

Shaped like a volcanic crater, this stadium was built for the 1968 Summer Olympics, and features a mosaic mural by Diego Rivera over the main entrance. The stadium holds 80,000 people.
Continue south. Take the Anillo Periférico, also known as La Ruta de la Amistad (Friendship Blvd), and take the turning to Xochimilco.

3 Xochimilco Ecological Park and Floating Gardens

This newly redesigned 230ha (568 acres) ecological park has 14km (8¾ miles) of canals open to the public. Its many gardens make it a true nature retreat within one of the world's largest cities. The recreational area includes bicycle rides and a tour through the park by train. There is also a Visitor Information Centre. Walk through the Paseo de las Flores, a showplace of colourful flowers, exotic plants and birds. The Botanical Gardens and Bird Reserve contain original flora and fauna and species of migratory birds from North America. Lago Acitlalin in the Botanical Gardens can be enjoyed by pedal boats. Visit Jardin Xochitla, where, on eight hectares (20 acres) of *chinampas,* you can watch a demonstration of this form of cultivation on floating gardens in the ancient style of India. End your visit with a relaxing ride on a *trajinera,* a flower-festooned shaded punt on Lago Huetzalin.
Open: Tue–Sun 9am–6pm.
Tel: (55) 5673 8061.

Take the Anillo Periférico northwest, cross over Insurgentes Sur, and turn right on to the Paseo del Pedregal. Continue north.

4 Jardines del Pedregal

Formerly a volcanic wasteland, Jardines del Pedregal has been transformed into a smart residential area. Clever architecture has made use of lava shapes and incorporated them into houses and gardens.
Take Avenida San Jerónimo northeast, and then follow Avenida Revolución into San Angel district.

5 San Angel Colonial Residential Area

This is a charming area of colonial houses and cobblestone streets. Take a look at the old Carmelite convent (No 4), now the Museo de Carmen, with its flower-filled courtyard. Built in 1615–17, it contains an important collection of religious art, particularly Baroque sculptures; the crypt contains mummified bodies.

Nearby is the Plaza San Jacinto, a large square where every Saturday sees the Bazar Sábado. This is a vast craft centre, with stalls set up on the square itself and in surrounding buildings. Handicrafts come from all over Mexico, and the standard is high. While here, have a meal or a drink at the San Angel Inn, a beautifully restored 18th-century *hacienda* in Altavista.
Turn west on to the Anillo Periférico, and return north to Mexico City.

The Aztecs

According to legend, the Aztecs originated from the mythical Aztlán, believed to be the tiny island of Mexcaltitán, on the northwest coast of Mexico. The Aztecs, or Mexica, as they also called themselves, wandered long before arriving in the Valley of Mexico (Anáhuac) during the course of the 12th century AD. They settled in Chapultepec (Hill of the Grasshoppers) until around 1325 when, following a prophecy of their god Huitzilopochtli, they saw an eagle on a cactus eating a snake in the middle of Lake Texcoco, and founded their capital Tenochtitlán there.

Mosaic of the Aztec calendar in Taxco

The Aztecs went to battle against their neighbouring city states, and by 1428 had formed a triple alliance with the towns of Tlacopan and Texcoco, gradually establishing their supremacy in the Valley of Mexico. As their empire expanded, they constructed impressive buildings and excelled in artistic accomplishments. They also introduced new educational systems.

Religion played an important part in the development of the arts. The Aztecs believed they lived in the 'fifth world', the previous four having been destroyed by catastrophes. The most famous expression of their mythology is the impressive Stone of the Fifth Sun, commonly known as the Aztec Calendar. Discovered in Mexico City's Zócalo in 1790, it is displayed in the National Museum of Anthropology in Mexico City (*see pp34–5*).

Their foremost deities included Huitzilopochtli (their patron god), Tonatiuh (the sun god), Tezcatlipoca (the smoking mirror), and Quetzalcóatl (the plumed serpent). Their gods were appeased with human sacrifice, which the Aztecs practised on an even greater scale than previous civilisations.

They had a hierarchical social structure. The emperor, known as

Diego Rivera's mural of the market district of Tlatelolco in the great city of Tenochtitlán

tlatoani (he who speaks), was not hereditary but was selected by a small group of electors, who then became his council of advisors. Members of the administration, judiciary and army were called *tecuhtli*, and these posts were held for life. On a par with them were the priests. Beneath them but also held in high esteem were craftsmen.

By the time Moctezuma II ascended the throne at the beginning of the 16th century, the Aztecs had developed a rich and powerful empire with extensive dominions. Heavy taxes were levied on neighbouring states, causing resentment and enmity, and it was this that made these groups join the Spaniards in the eventual overthrow of the Aztec empire (*see pp14–15*).

Tour: Holy places and pyramids

This classic tour includes the Plaza of the Three Cultures, the Shrine of Guadalupe – the most venerated place in Mexico – and the famous archaeological site at Teotihuacán. A full day is recommended.

Start from Alameda Central and take Paseo de la Reforma travelling north. Turn left on to the Calzada Nonoalco to the Plaza de las Tres Culturas.

1 Plaza de las Tres Culturas

This square, in the city's northern district of Tlatelolco, features contrasting buildings from Mexico's three eras of history: pre-Columbian, Spanish Colonial and Modern. Aztec remains mark the spot of their final defeat by Cortés. The 17th-century Templo de Santiago in the middle of the square is an example of Spanish architecture, and the tall building of the Foreign Ministry from the 20th century serves as a sharp contrast.

Rejoin Reforma and continue along the Calzada de Guadalupe to the Basilica.

2 Basílica de Nuestra Señora de Guadalupe

The original basilica has been joined alongside by this striking modern building designed by Mexico's celebrated architect Pedro Ramírez Vázquez. Consecrated in 1976, it is one of Latin America's most venerated shrines and Mexico's most important place of pilgrimage *(see p32)*. Pilgrims – some on their knees – make their way across the courtyard on the final stage of their journey. Inside, a moving walkway takes visitors slowly past the famous cloak bearing the image of the Virgin.

Take Insurgentes Norte (R85). Turn off east to Acolman.

3 Monastery of Acolman

This is a fine, 16th-century Augustinian monastery in peaceful surroundings. Its façade is in plateresque style, while inside are some attractive murals and golden retablos. The beautiful cloisters surround a small grove of orange trees.

Continue north for a short distance and follow the signs to San Juan Teotihuacán.

4 Pyramids of Teotihuacán

This ancient ceremonial centre of pyramids, palaces and broad avenues is positively grandiose (*see pp8–9*). While early structures are thought to date back to 100 BC, little is known of its origins. At the southernmost entrance to the site, a small museum traces the history and development of Teotihuacán (there are son-et-lumière performances in the evenings, except on Mondays, subject to the weather).

The first structure, the Ciudadela (Citadel), centres around the Temple of Quetzalcóatl, noted for its sculptured serpents and masks. From here, a broad street, the Avenue of the Dead, extends northwards for 4km (2½ miles), passing in front of the Pyramid of the Sun and ending at the Pyramid of the Moon. Designed and positioned with remarkable precision, these demonstrate the depth of astronomical knowledge achieved by the Teotihuacános. The climb up steps and platforms is rewarded with excellent views of the complex. The Pyramid of the Moon is much smaller than that of the Sun, but of equal height, being set on higher ground. Another structure of interest is the completely restored Palace of Quetzalpapálotl, part of the priests' residential complex.

Head for Tecamac and rejoin R85 to return to Mexico City.

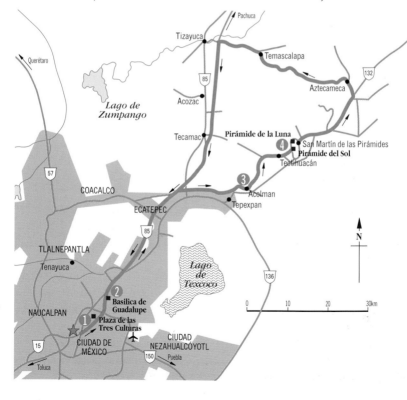

Tour: Holy places and pyramids

Central Mexico and the southern Gulf

This area includes the central highlands around Mexico City, extending south to the state of Oaxaca, and eastward to the Gulf of Mexico. Within the region lies an enormous diversity of climates, landscapes and cultures.

The central areas are characterised by great pine forests, lakes and mountains. South of this, the landscape is dominated by the snow-capped volcanoes that form the volcanic range extending from the Pacific coast to Veracruz on the Gulf of Mexico. It includes the active volcano of Popocatépetl. The range gives way to the rugged mountains and valleys of Oaxaca, which contrast with the humid tropical jungles of the Gulf region. This central region – the most populous area of Mexico and also of great economic importance – offers countless attractions. Three hundred years of

The 5,452m (17,887ft) high Popocatépetl (Smoking Mountain) is an active volcano and is sometimes closed to climbers

Spanish rule resulted in colonial towns, magnificent churches, charming old *haciendas* (now converted into hotels) and tranquil spa resorts.

Surviving from an earlier era are numerous archaeological sites, vestiges of the Aztec, Toltec and other pre-Columbian cultures. Oaxaca, with its large, indigenous population, is known for its markets, pottery and weaving. This region was once the centre of the ancient Zapotec and Mixtec cultures. Among the pre-Hispanic sites in the area, the most important are Monte Albán and Mitla.

The cradle of Mexican civilisation, however, is to be found in the Gulf basin, where the Olmecs developed the mother culture at La Venta. This is a region of dense jungle, tropical flowers and fragrant plantations of tobacco, coffee and vanilla.

Central Mexico and the southern Gulf

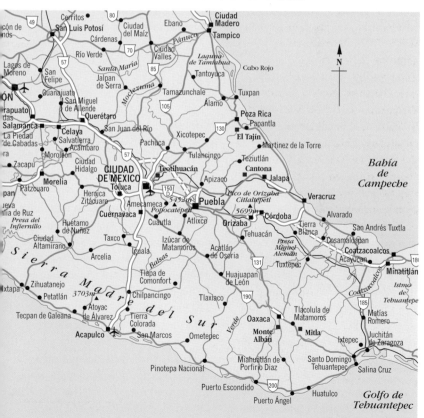

Walk the planks, down a wooden jetty, to choose your touring vessel at Lake Chapala

Chapala

This popular little resort town stands on the northern shores of Laguna de Chapala, the largest lake in Mexico. Its agreeable year-round climate is one of the factors that, for many years, has attracted foreign residents, especially from North America. Chapala – although close to Guadalajara, Mexico's second-largest city – still maintains its tranquillity.

The town has a pleasant promenade along the lakeshore, with lively bars and restaurants and *mariachi* musicians, who usually charge for their songs these days (part of the fun is to drive a bargain). Launches are available for hire, as well as equipment for watersports. Along the lake to the west are the quaint little towns of Ajijic and Jocotepec, renowned for handicrafts and weaving.

42km (26 miles) south of Guadalajara. There are several daily bus services from the Central Camionera (Central Bus Station). The journey takes about 45 minutes.

Cholula

It is said that Cholula has a church for every day of the year. While the reality may fall well short of this, there are enough churches to serve a major metropolis. One of the most impressive is the 16th-century Franciscan San Gabriel Church on the *zócalo*. The Royal Chapel, once attended by great numbers of Indians, is remarkable for its huge atrium. The *zócalo* itself is large and handsome. Cholula is the seat of the University of the Americas.

Most visitors come to see the great Pyramid of Tepanapa, said to be the largest structure of its kind in the world (though not the tallest). It was once an important trading centre, and had religious ties with various cultures from the Olmecs to the Aztecs. Guided tours explore part of its vast network of tunnels. Crowning the site is the Spanish-built Church of Nuestra Señora de los Remedios.

12km (7¹/₂ miles) west of Puebla, by bus, car or taxi. Pyramid, Zona Arqueológica. Open: daily Tue–Sun 9am–6pm. Admission charge.

Cuernavaca

See pp74–5.

El Tajín

Lying northwest of Veracruz amid vanilla plantations bordering forested slopes are the extensive ruins of El Tajín (which means 'lightning' in Totonac). While its early origins are uncertain, some experts now attribute the city to the Huastecs, while others surmise the founders were of Mayan lineage. It later developed as the ceremonial capital of the Totonacs, reaching its height of power between AD 900 and 1100,

when most of its finest buildings were constructed. The place was later abandoned and lost to the jungle.

The site is dominated by the Pyramid of the Niches, a magnificent structure of six storeys topped by a temple. A broad stairway runs up the main façade, while around the sides are 365 niches, representing the days of the year. Two Ball Courts can be seen in this area; the south court has six panels showing various rituals. A walk up the path leads to the Plaza of Tajín Chico. The Building of the Columns, which features great columns adorned with carvings, offers a fine view from the top, good for watching the dramatic spectacle of the Flying Men of Papantla, who perform for tourists (*see p80*).

20km (12¹/₂ miles) southeast of Poza Rica. Open: daily 8am–6pm. Admission charge. By air from Mexico City to Poza Rica, then bus or taxi. Bus services from Mexico City to Poza Rica leave from the Terminal Central Norte.

Central Mexico and the southern Gulf

El Tajín's Pyramid of the God of Death (right) and the tiered Pyramid of the Niches (left)

Guadalajara

Guadalajara is Mexico's second city, the capital of Jalisco state. It is a fast-developing metropolis that nevertheless retains its colonial heritage, with parks and fountains surrounded by mansions. The 16th-century, twin-towered **Catedral** is an impressive structure flanked by four main squares arranged like a cross. Great works by José Clemente Orozco (1883–1949), one of Mexico's leading muralists, can be seen in the **Palacio de Gobierno** (Government Palace). More can be seen in the **Instituto Cultural Cabañas** cultural centre, which houses the *Four Horsemen of the Apocalypse.*

Guadalajara is the home of the famous *mariachi* musicians; hear them at the Plaza de los Mariachis. In the surrounding areas *tequila* is produced, and the suburb of Tlaquepaque is a top crafts centre (*see p149*).

586km (364 miles) west of Mexico City. Information office: Sectur, Morelos 102, Plaza Tapatía. Tel: (3) 668 1600, Mon–Fri 8am–6pm & Sat–Sun 9am–1pm. Regular flights from Mexico City, other domestic destinations, and the US. Rail and bus services from the north and Mexico City.

GUADALAJARA

Catedral Plaza de la Liberación.
Tel: (33) 3614 5504.
Open: daily 8am–8pm.

Instituto Cultural Cabañas Calle Cabañas 8.
Tel: (33) 3818 2800, ext 31014. Open: Tue–Sat 10am–6pm, Sun 10am–3pm. Admission charge.

Palacio del Gobierno Plaza de Armas.
Tel: (33) 3668 1800. Open: weekdays 9am–8pm.

Teatro Degollado Plaza de la Liberación.
Tel: (33) 3614 4773. Open for viewing theatre, Mon–Fri 12.30–2.30pm.

GUANAJUATO

Alhóndiga de Granaditas Calle de 28 de Septiembre. *Tel: (473) 732 1112.* Open: Tue–Sat 10am–2pm, 4–6pm, Sun 10am–3pm. Admission charge.

Museo de las Momías
Explanada del Panteón Municipal.
Tel: (473) 732 0639. Open: daily 9am–6pm. Admission charge.

Museo Diego Rivera Positos 47. *Tel: (473) 732 1197.* Open: Tue–Sat 10am–6.30pm, Sun 10am–2.30pm. Admission charge.

Guanajuato

The old mining town of Guanajuato is one of Mexico's most attractive colonial towns, tucked away among a ring of hills. With beautiful old houses painted in many colours, crooked cobblestone streets winding up the hillsides, attractive squares and unique subterranean streets, it is a town best explored on foot (*see pp56–7*).

In the 1700s, Guanajuato was the prosperous centre of a rich mining area. La Valenciana became one of the richest silver-producing mines in the world (still operating today).

This was the first important town to be taken by the Mexicans in the Independence War. A local miner lost his life after setting on fire the massive gates of the **Alhóndiga de Granaditas** (granary), where the Spaniards had taken refuge. When Hidalgo and Allende, leaders of the movement, were captured and killed by the Spaniards, their heads were displayed in the granary, which is now a museum. Just outside town is the catacomb-like **Museo de las Momias**, with dozens of excellently preserved mummies.

The city is home to one of Mexico's foremost universities. Strolling musicians from the university, known as *estudiantinas*, add to the lively atmosphere. This is also the birthplace of renowned muralist Diego Rivera.

His former home is now a museum.

The gigantic El Pípila monument on San Miguel Hill offers a magnificent view of the town. The nearby Valenciana church is a stunning Churrigueresque building, and the famous mine is across the road. Another trip of interest is to the colossal Christ the King statue on Cubilete Hill.

376km (234 miles) northwest of Mexico City. Information office: Sectur, Plaza de la Paz. Free tel: (01 800) 714 1086. Flights from Mexico City and US destinations. Bus and rail services from Mexico City and other towns.

Guadalajara

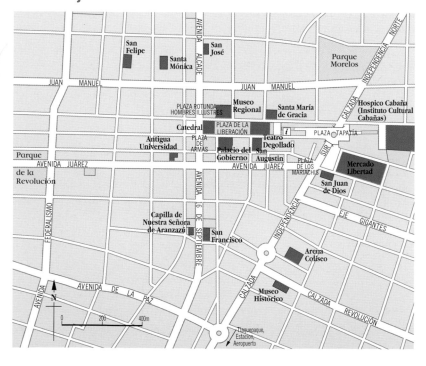

Walk: Guanajuato

For this walk through the cultural heart of beautiful colonial Guanajuato (see pp54–5), wear comfortable shoes for the cobblestone streets and watch out for the very busy traffic.

Allow 3 hours.

Start from the Plaza Dr Romero. Take a look at the fine façade of the 18th-century Templo de San Francisco (Church of St Francis), and walk up the left side of the Calle Sopena to the museum.

1 Museo Iconográfico del Quijote

This extraordinary Iconographic Museum of Don Quixote, opened in 1987, has a collection of almost 600 works, donated by the Spaniard Señor

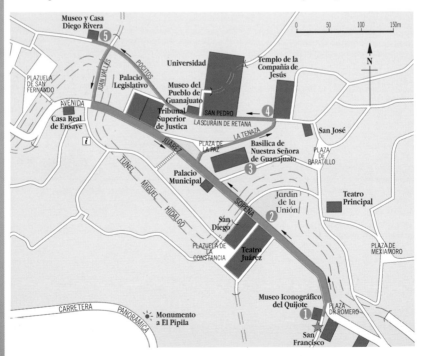

Eulalio Ferrier, relating to Miguel de Cervantes' famous character. Its many rooms contain paintings, lithographs and sculptures of this famous fictional hero. There are also works by Picasso and Dalí.

Tel: (473) 732 3376. Open: Tue–Sat 10am–6.30pm, Sun 10am–2pm. Closed: Mon. Admission charge.

Continue up Calle Sopena. On your left you will pass the splendid Teatro Juárez (Juárez Theatre), followed by the Templo de San Diego (St James's Church). Behind is the Casa de las Artesanías (Arts and Crafts Centre). Continue up to Jardín de la Unión.

2 Jardín de la Unión

Union Garden is a lovely square, a focal point of Guanajuato with laurel trees, benches, and cafés and restaurants lining one side. It is always lively, a favourite meeting place for locals and students, and in the evenings musicians perform here.

Proceed up to the Plaza de la Paz to the Basílica.

3 Basílica de Nuestra Señora de Guanajuato

Our Lady of Guanajuato is an imposing 17th-century Baroque basilica, atop a flight of steps. Inside is a much-revered statue of the Virgin donated in 1557 by King Philip II of Spain.

Go round to the left of the basilica and down La Tenaza until you reach the Jesuit Church.

4 Templo de la Compañía de Jesús

This 18th-century Jesuit Church, which holds a commanding position on a hilltop, is noted for its magnificent Churrigueresque façade in pink stone. The somewhat austere interior features a red-brick ceiling, Guanajuato-style, and statues of saints in the niches.

Turn right from the church and walk up Calle San Pedro Lascuráin de Retana. On your right you will pass an impressive flight of steps leading up to the Universidad de Guanajuato. On your left are cafés, bars and restaurants. Continue along Calle Pocitos, passing the local Museo del Pueblo de Guanajuato to a Venetian red house marked No 47, which is the Museo y Casa de Diego Rivera.

5 Museo y Casa de Diego Rivera

Mexico's great muralist was born in this house in 1886, and spent his childhood here. Furniture and old photographs offer a glimpse of his everyday life. The museum displays some of his works and sketches, as well as sculptures and exhibits of other artists.

Tel: (473) 732 1197. Open: Tue–Sat 10am–6.30pm, Sun 10am–2.30pm. Closed: Mon. Admission charge.

Turn left back down Pocitos, continuing right down Calle Juan Valles, then left, passing the splendid Palacio Legislativo on your left. There are shops on your right. Round the walk off with a drink at the Plaza de la Paz.

Mitla

One of the foremost archaeological sites in the state of Oaxaca, Mitla belongs to the Zapotec and Mixtec civilisations, and is renowned for its magnificent mosaic work adorning the buildings (attributed to the Mixtecs). The site is just off the main square of the tiny village of Mitla, which bustles with stalls and vendors selling colourful traditional clothes, woven rugs, basketware and local handicrafts.

Mitla's first inhabitants were the Zapotecs, and by the 1st century AD it had become an important religious centre. Around the 10th century, the Mixtecs arrived from the central region of Mexico, and their culture reached its peak in the 13th century. Mitla gets its name from a Náhuatl word meaning 'Place of the Dead', after the burial grounds there, but it has also inherited the name 'Place of Palaces' after its masterfully ornamented buildings of the Mixtecs, known as the Cloud People. Skilled artisans, they produced beautiful structures covered with fine ornamentation in geometric patterns of coils and keys to depict a stylised plumed serpent – among other religious symbols.

Unlike many other archaeological sites that have been uncovered, Mitla stands largely intact, and relatively little restoration has been necessary. It covers a fairly small area and is divided into five groups, of which only two have been fully excavated.

The most important is the Grupo de las Columnas, a group of columns built around two patios. The Salón de las Columnas features six large columns; from here a narrow passageway leads to the Patio de las Grecas, also known as the Fret Patio on account of the geometric patterns on the walls.

OTHER ARCHAEOLOGICAL SITES

Between Mitla and Oaxaca are several smaller Zapotec sites. Near Mitla are the Zapotec ruins of Yagul ('Old Hill'). The major structure is the Palacio de los Seis Patios (Palace of the Six Courtyards). Nearer Oaxaca are the sites of Lambityeco and Dainzú, partly excavated.

Yagul
Open: daily 8am–6pm.

Lambityeco
Open: daily 8am–5pm.

Dainzú
Open: daily 8am–5pm.
Small admission charge for each site (Sun free).

This is the highlight of the site, displaying the exquisite workmanship of the Mixtec artisans, who used thousands of cut stones to make up the intricate mosaic pattern. In front of the complex is the mosaic-decorated entrance to an underground tomb. The Columna de la Vida (Column of Life) in front of the entrance is supposed to measure life expectancy, as calculated by the distance that is left after placing your arms around the column.

Second in importance is the Grupo de la Iglesia (Church Group), also with richly adorned buildings. Then there is the Grupo del Sur (South Group), and, to the west, the Grupo del Arroyo (Stream Group) and the Grupo de los Adobos (Adobe Group).

Mitla ruins: 38km (23½ miles) southeast of Oaxaca. Open: 9am–5pm. Admission charge (Sun & holidays free). Most people take a tour from Oaxaca. This usually includes a stop to admire the Tule Tree, an extraordinary giant ahuehuete, having a circumference of 57m (62yds) (the largest in the world), and believed to be about 2,500 years old.

THE MUSEO FRISSELL DE ARTE ZAPOTECA

The Frissell Museum, just off the main square, has a fine collection of Zapotec and Mixtec artefacts. Open: daily 9am–6pm. Free admission.

The Tule Tree, already old at the time of Christ

Monte Albán

Monte Albán ('White Mountain') is Oaxaca's top attraction. Built on a flat hilltop with a spectacular view of the mountains and broad valley of Oaxaca, this is one of Mexico's foremost archaeological sites, and a major testimony to the Zapotec and Mixtec civilisations.

Monte Albán's origins are not known, although there is evidence to suggest influences of the Olmec La Venta culture. Between about 600 BC and AD 1200, it was developed in distinct stages by the Zapotecs, and it grew to become an important religious centre with a population peaking at 25,000. After this time Monte Albán fell into decline, and was gradually abandoned by the Zapotecs. Around AD 1300, it was taken over by the Mixtecs, who used it as burial grounds for their dignitaries.

A path up the hillside from the car park leads to the entrance on the northeast corner. Here, you will be met by the grandeur of the Gran Plaza, a vast grassy area surrounded by great solid structures, with a group of buildings in the centre. Stairways and platforms enable you to scramble up and down the temples with relative ease.

Down on your left is the Ball Court; however, no stone rings can be seen, as with other Ball Courts in the Oaxaca region. Over to your right is the impressive Plataforma Norte (North Platform), which offers a magnificent view from the top. Continuing anticlockwise, you will pass another monument, which is known simply as Sistema IV (System IV), before arriving at one of the most interesting sections of the complex. Los Danzantes (The Dancers) are a set of stelae with figures carved in strange dance-like positions. There are many different theories as to the significance of these

BALL GAMES

To the peoples of pre-Conquest Mexico, the innocent-sounding 'ball game' (known as *tlachtli*) was both a religious ritual and a form of recreation. The solid rubber ball was kept in constant motion in the air by the players using only their elbows, hips or knees, mimicking the movements of the heavenly bodies, and perhaps itself symbolising the sun or moon. The finale was frequently a gruesome human sacrifice: either the loser was decapitated and his head possibly used as a ball, or he was tortured to death, and his body trussed up into a ball shape by the victor and bounced down the steps of the pyramid.

figures, which show deformities and – judging by their features – a strong Olmec influence.

At the far end of the Gran Plaza is the Plataforma Sur (South Platform), largest of the structures. A climb to the top of the platform will give you an excellent view of the site and its surrounding hills.

From here you can walk across to the central buildings. The arrow-shaped Montículo (Mound) is one of the earliest and most complex structures to be found here. Adjacent is another group known as Edificios (Buildings) G, H and I. To the right is the building known as El Palacio (The Palace),

where a passageway leads to an impressive patio, indicating that the temple may have been used to house dignitaries. Of interest, too, are the tombs located beyond the North Platform. In 1932, priceless treasures were found in some of these, especially Tombs 7 and 104, which can be seen in Oaxaca's Regional State Museum. Archaeologist Dr Alfonso Caso, honoured by a monument at the entrance, discovered some 50 tombs here during the course of his work.

6km (3³/4 miles) west of Oaxaca. Tel: (951) 516 1215. Open: daily 8am–6pm. Admission charge (Sun & holidays free). Best visited by tour from Oaxaca.

The Ball Court at Monte Albán

Oaxaca

The clarity of its skies and its setting, amid mountains, its churches, museums, handicrafts, markets and ambience, give the state capital a special attraction. Oaxaca combines colonial architecture with an indigenous population. It also serves as a base for excursions to the major ruins and colourful Indian markets in the region.

The *zócalo* (*see p64*) is the focal point of life in Oaxaca. Closed to traffic, it has neatly laid trees, inviting benches and an elegant bandstand where rousing concerts are held, all surrounded by arcades and cafés. Sunday is especially enjoyable, with Indian women weaving and selling their wares. For the very daring, they also offer an unusual culinary experience: bowls of fried grasshoppers or live worms. The Mercado de Abastos is Oaxaca's famed daily market southwest of the town. It is at its liveliest and most colourful on Saturdays.

On the north side of the *zócalo* stands the cathedral. Started in 1533 and completed 200 years later, it has a fine Baroque façade of greenish stone, and a clock donated by the King of Spain. A few blocks away is Oaxaca's most impressive church, the 16th-century **Templo de Santo Domingo de Guzmán** (*see p65*). Its rich interior, gilded and painted by Mexican craftsmen, is one of the most significant in the country. Not far from here is the **Basílica de la Virgen de la Soledad**, with a jewel-encrusted statue of the Virgin. Housed in the monastery of Santo Domingo, the **Museo Regional de Oaxaca** (*see p65*) has a rich collection of artefacts, including treasures from the tombs of Monte Albán. The nearby **Museo Rufino Tamayo** (*see p65*) has a fine collection of pre-Columbian works donated by the renowned local artist himself.

523km (325 miles) southeast of Mexico City. Tourist office: Avenida Independencia 603. Tel: (951) 516 0123. Frequent flights and regular bus connections from Mexico City and other towns.

OAXACA
Basílica de la Virgen de la Soledad Avenida de la Independencia.
Tel: (951) 516 7566.
Open: daily 7am–7pm.

Museo Regional de Oaxaca
Plaza Santo Domingo.
Tel: (951) 516 2991.
Open: Tue–Sun 10am–7pm.
Admission charge.

Museo Rufino Tamayo Avenida Morelos.
Tel: (951) 516 4750.
Open: Mon–Sat 10am–2pm, 4–7pm, Sun 10am–3pm. Admission charge.

Templo de Santo Domingo de Guzmán Calle Macedonio Alcalá and Calle A Gurrión.
Tel: (951) 516 3720.
Open: daily 7am–1pm & 4–8pm.

PATZCUARO
Basílica de Nuestra Señora de la Salud
Calle Lerín.

Museo de Artes Populares Calle Lerín. Open: Tue–Sat 9am–7pm, Sun 9am–4.30pm. Admission charge.

Orizaba

Orizaba makes an attractive stop on the way to the city of Veracruz, mainly for its lush setting with stunning views of Pico de Orizaba, Mexico's highest volcano. *276km (171 miles) southeast of Mexico City. Regular bus service from Mexico City and Veracruz.*

Pátzcuaro

This quaint little town in the west of Mexico's central region is the heartland of the Tarascan Indians. Fishing, farming and handicrafts are the main means of livelihood. The town is one of cobblestone streets and red-roofed houses. Its most attractive feature is the park-like Plaza Principal Vasco de Quiroga, with a fountain, ash trees and handsome buildings surrounding it. Places of interest include the Casa del Gigante (House of the Giant) on the square, and the small shopping centre of Casa de los Once Patios (House of Eleven Patios). The **Museo de Artes Populares**, housed in the former Colegio de San Nicolás, displays masks, textiles, local pottery, copper, lacquerware and straw figures. One block north of this Museum of Popular Art, the **Basílica de Nuestra Señora de la Salud** (Our Lady of Health) – built in 1554 and rebuilt in 1883 – contains a celebrated cornpaste image of the Virgin Mary.

Many visitors make the trip to nearby Lake Pátzcuaro – 10 minutes by bus or taxi to the jetty. Restaurants line the marina, and boats can take you across to **Janitzio** (a 40-minute journey). This tiny island rises up like a cone, with picturesque little houses and terraced steps leading up to a gigantic statue of José María Morelos, hero of the War of Independence. Janitzio is rustic, and crammed with restaurants, stalls and handicraft shops all the way up. The climb is steep, but worth it for the view.

Janitzio is famed for its Festival of the Day of the Dead (*see p21*). *Pátzcuaro is 365km (227 miles) west of Mexico City. There are bus services from Morelia and other destinations.*

The jewel of Oaxaca, the interior of the exquisite church of Santo Domingo de Guzmán

Central Mexico and the southern Gulf

Walk: Oaxaca

A UNESCO Heritage for Humanity site, Oaxaca is a town for leisurely strolls. This walk through the centre includes a look at its major colonial attractions, combined with the flavour of its indigenous population (see p62).

Allow 3 hours.

Start at the zócalo (main square).

1 Zócalo

This beautiful square, surrounded by arcades, is the hub of Oaxaca, and a marvellous place for lingering in one of the many cafés and restaurants to watch the non-stop activity – local

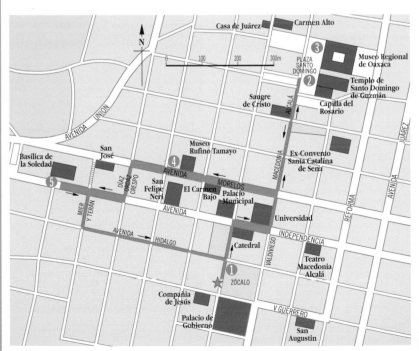

women with long, dark plaits and colourful costumes, the ubiquitous vendors, and comings and goings of musicians. The square leads to an adjoining square which is dominated on its northern side by the cathedral. *Pass by the cathedral, turn right along Avenida Independencia, cross over and take Calle Macedonia Alcalá, a pedestrian street with houses painted in different colours, a few shops and markets. You will pass the Casa de Cortés, which now houses the city museum. Continue to the Plaza Santo Domingo on your right.*

2 Templo de Santo Domingo de Guzmán

On this large, open plaza adorned by strikingly flamboyant trees stands St Dominic's Church. Founded in the late 16th century, its vaulted ceiling is inset with 36 paintings by local craftsmen. Of special note is the genealogical tree of the Guzmáns, the family of Domingo de Guzmán, 13th-century founder of the Dominican Order.
Adjoining is the Museo Regional de Oaxaca.

3 Museo Regional de Oaxaca

Housed in the former monastery (Ex-Convento) of Santo Domingo, Oaxaca's regional museum is a beautiful building of grand cloisters. The fine collection includes artefacts from the Zapotec and Mixtec cultures. Outstanding are the objects of gold, crystal and other

material found in Tomb 7 in Monte Albán, displayed in a special room on the left as you enter.

Nearby are some attractive shops. Across from the museum, the Palacio de Santo Domingo shopping centre offers a wide variety of colourful handicrafts. In the Oro de Monte Albán, you can buy excellent reproductions of the Mixtec gold jewellery from Tomb 7. You can also watch goldsmiths at work.
Return down Macedonia Alcalá and turn right along Avenida Morelos to the Museo Rufino Tamayo.

4 Museo Rufino Tamayo

Rufino Tamayo, considered one of Mexico's great artists, was a native of Oaxaca. He died in 1991 at the age of 91. This lovely old colonial mansion contains a collection of pre-Columbian treasures and other pieces from his private collection.
Take Díaz Ordáz Crespo and turn right along Avenida Independencia to the Basílica de la Soledad.

5 Basílica de la Soledad

This is another of Oaxaca's lovely churches, built in the 17th century. Inside is the graceful figure of Our Lady of Solitude, the city's patron saint. Note the vast gold crown adorned with diamonds that she wears. Behind the church is a small museum devoted to the Virgin.
Turn down Mier Y Teran and left on to Avenida Hidalgo, back to the zócalo.

Puebla

Watched over by four snow-topped volcanoes – Orizaba, Popocatépetl, Iztaccíhuatl and the smaller La Malinche – Puebla is Mexico's fourth-largest town and a thriving commercial centre. The town was laid out by the Spaniards, who introduced the art of tile-making, and its churches and façades, adorned with Talavera tiles, speak eloquently of those colonial days.

Puebla has many fine churches. The vast **catedral** (*see p68*), located on the south side of the main square, is considered one of the most important in Mexico. Built between the mid-16th and 18th centuries, it has a rather austere Renaissance-style façade, and some 14 chapels. Nearby, the 17th-century **Templo de Santo Domingo** (*see pp68–9*) is noted for its Capilla del Rosario (Rosary Chapel), one of Mexico's masterpieces. Other notable places include the **Museo Amparo**, famed for its fine collection of pre-Hispanic and colonial art, and the richly tiled **Casa del Alfeñique** (Sugarcake House). The latter is Puebla's regional museum, and features archaeological artefacts, historical relics and regional crafts.

One street behind the Museo Amparo you will find the Plaza de los Sapos, an enchanting square, filled with pleasant bars and pavement cafés, where antique and crafts open-air markets take place every Saturday. Just two blocks away, don't miss El Parian, a long, richly decorated passageway crammed with

PUEBLA
Catedral Calle 16 de Séptiembre. *Tel: (222) 243 9395.* Open: 7am–12.30pm, 4.15–7.30pm.
Museo Regional (Casa del Alfeñique) Calle 6 Norte. *Tel: (222) 232 4296.* Open: Tue–Sun 10am–5pm. Admission charge.
Templo de Santo Domingo Bulevar Heroes del 5 de mayo. *Tel: (222) 242 3643.* Open: Mon–Sat 7.30am–1pm, 4–8pm; Sun 7.30am–8pm.
Museo Amparo Calle 2 Sur. *Tel: (222) 229 3850.* Open: Wed–Mon 10am–6pm. Admission charge.

QUERETARO
Museo Regional Corregidora 3 Sur. *Tel: (442) 212 2031.* Open: Tue–Sun 10am–7pm. Admission charge.

SAN MIGUEL DE ALLENDE
Iglesia Parroquial Calle Correo. *Tel: (415) 152 0544.* Open: Tue–Sat 10am–4pm, Sun 10am–2pm.
Museo Casa de Don Ignacio Allende Cuna de Allende 1. *Tel: (415) 152 2499.* Open: Mon–Fri 9am–6pm, Sat 9am–1pm.

shops selling fine Talavera pottery, textile goods and other fine crafts.

Lying 97km (60 miles) east of Puebla is the newly excavated site of Cantona, believed to date from the 8th century AD. Built into the hillside, it covers a large area containing ceremonial structures and Ball Courts.

126km (78 miles) southeast of Mexico City. Tourist office: 5 Oriente No 3. Tel: (222) 246 2044. Frequent buses from Mexico City and other centres.

Querétaro

Querétaro is often bypassed by visitors in their rush to reach the more obvious

The aqueduct at Querétaro was built in 1726 and is nearly 10km (6¼ miles) long

attractions of Guanajuato and San Miguel de Allende. But within the industrial outskirts lies a fine historic town with a colonial centre, small plazas and fine stone buildings with intricate wrought-iron work. It also features an old aqueduct, and is known for its opals and semi-precious stones.

Main squares are the Plaza de Armas, Jardín Obregón and the Jardín de la Corregidora, where a statue honours 'La Corregidora', Josefa Ortíz de Domínguez, who warned Father Hidalgo and the other conspirators plotting against Spain of their imminent arrest. Other churches and buildings of interest include the Templo de Santa Rosa de Viterbo, the Templo de Santa Clara and the **Museo Regional**, which is housed in the 17th-century Franciscan monastery.

A short trip northwest of the centre takes you to the Cerro de las Campanas (Hill of Bells), where a flight of steps set in attractive gardens leads up to a tiny chapel. This marks the site of Emperor Maximilian's execution by a firing squad. On the brow of the hill stands a huge, menacing statue of the man who ordered his death, Benito Juárez.

213km (132 miles) north of Mexico City. Tourist office: Pasteur 4 Norte, Plaza Independencia. Tel: (442) 238 5067; (01 800) 715 1742. There are bus and rail services from Mexico City and other destinations.

San Miguel de Allende

This little town, with its steep cobblestone streets, hidden courtyards and a magnificent church, is a national monument. It is dominated by the **Iglesia Parroquial** (parish church), a huge 19th-century Neo-Gothic structure in pink stone. Below it, surrounded by arcades, is the pretty little *zócalo*. The centre is compact and filled with art galleries, boutiques and handicrafts for which the town is renowned. The **Museo Casa de Don Ignacio Allende** is a well-established art centre housed in a beautiful 18th-century mansion.

286km (178 miles) north of Mexico City. Tourist office: Plaza de Allende. Tel: (415) 152 0900. www.turismosanmiguel.com.mx. Buses from Mexico City and other centres.

Tour: The Route of the Churches

This tour in and around Puebla takes you to some of Mexico's most interesting and unusual churches whose artistic vision combines the best of colonial and Indian skills.

Allow 3 hours.

Start in the main square, Plaza de la Constitución, and walk over to the cathedral on the south side.

1 Catedral

This vast structure, the second largest in Mexico, has a rather austere look. Started in 1575, it took 100 years to complete. Relief figures on the north doorway depict the four Spanish Habsburg kings – Charles V and Philips II, III and IV. The style is part Baroque, part Renaissance.

Tel: (222) 243 9395. Open: 7am–12.30pm & 4.15–7.30pm. Cross the lively zócalo *and take the* ramblas, *Cinco de Mayo, on the other side, to the Templo de Santo Domingo on the left.*

2 Templo de Santo Domingo

St Dominic's Church dates back to the early 17th century and has a Baroque

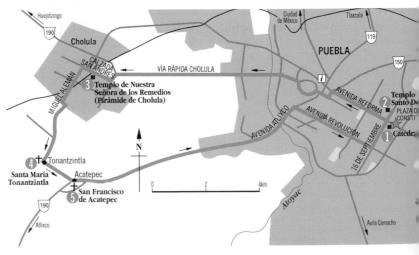

façade. Inside is a veritable jewel, the Capilla del Rosario (Rosary Chapel), gloriously decorated with gold leaf and sculptures. On a Sunday, you might well come across a christening or some other local event.

Tel: (222) 242 3643 (see p66).
Tourist information: Tel: (222) 246 2044.
info@turismopuebla.com.mx
Now walk back towards the main square and take a taxi for a little tour of the surroundings. Agree on a price, usually calculated by the hour. It takes about 15 minutes to the pyramid and church of Cholula.

3 Pirámide de Cholula and Templo de Nuestra Señora de los Remedios

This is the largest pyramid in the world in terms of circumference, topped by a charming little church with twin yellow towers. The pyramid dates back to before the Classic period of pre-Hispanic Mexico, and is believed to have been rebuilt over seven times. To visit the tunnels inside (where a small torch is useful), you must buy a ticket at the ticket window across the road.

It is possible to climb up to the church, which was built by the Spaniards in 1666, and rebuilt in the mid-19th century after it was damaged by an earthquake. There are wonderful views from both this spot and the hill opposite, with a magnificent backdrop provided by the snowy peak of the Orizaba volcano.

Open: Tue–Sun 9am–6pm. Admission charge.

Continue to the church of Santa María de Tonantzintla, located a few kilometres southwest, just outside the tiny village of the same name.

4 Santa María de Tonantzintla

This enchanting church was constructed in the 18th century by local Indians. The appealing exterior consists of a single tower, red and blue tiles, and honey-coloured side walls. Every inch of the interior is exuberantly covered by cherubs, fruit and other patterns.

About 2km (1¼ miles) further along is the Church of San Francisco de Acatepec.

5 San Francisco de Acatepec

This is another beauty. More sumptuous than the previous church, it has a magnificent façade tiled in typical *poblano* (Puebla) style in red, blue and yellow, with twin towers. The interior, which was also partly the work of Indians, is richly decorated, with an elaborate gilded altar.

Return to Puebla, 5km (3 miles) east.

Nuestra Señora de los Remedios

Tour: The Route of the Churches

Silver mining

The Spaniards who conquered Mexico in 1521 lusted after the gold of the Aztecs. Although initial explorations were disappointing, it was not long before rich veins of a different precious metal – silver – were discovered in the mountainous regions of Zacatecas, Guanajuato and Pachuca.

Silver mining then started in a big way. Zacatecas gradually became more prosperous until, by the beginning of the 17th century, it was one of the richest cities in Mexico. Silver also brought wealth to Guanajuato. The Valenciana Mine, established in 1766, became one of the world's most productive silver mines. Taxco, too, prospered after large deposits of silver were discovered nearby in the mid-18th century by Frenchman José de la Borda.

Vast quantities of silver, gold and other minerals shipped to Spain made an important contribution to the economy. Recovering from a fall in

A Taxco silversmith

El Pedgreal silver mine

silver production in the mid-1660s, Mexico became the world's top producer of silver by the end of the 17th century.

Slaves were employed in the mines, and living and working conditions of these Indian miners were very tough. Later, legislation improved matters and unions were formed.

Over time, however, gradual decline set in, mines closed down, and some old mining centres were abandoned to become ghost towns. Others, like the Valenciana Mine of Guanajuato, have been reactivated and continue in operation today. El Solar is one of several silver mines in operation around Taxco, where the town's flourishing silver industry earned it the nickname of Silver City. Hundreds of shops there display exquisitely wrought silverware and jewellery. Once again, Mexico ranks as among the world's foremost producers of silver.

Replica of Hernán Cortés' ship, the *Marigallante*

Taxco

The beauty of Taxco is legendary (see p75). Long declared a national monument, the town's old buildings are preserved, and new construction follows the colonial style.

Although silver had already been discovered earlier by the Spaniards, Taxco came to prominence in the early 1800s when French prospector and miner José de la Borda found a series of rich silver veins in the area. While accruing his own fortune, he also sponsored the construction of the superb church of Santa Prisca.

The silver industry had declined, however, by the time a New Orleans professor of architecture, Bill Spratling, came to Taxco in 1929 to write a book. He fell in love with the place, and trained the locals in silversmithing; as this developed into a profitable business, the demise of the town was halted. Taxco is now synonymous with silver.

high over the hills. To visit the El Solar silver mine on the outskirts of town, an appointment is needed.

164km (102 miles) south of Mexico City. Tourist office: Avenida de los Plateros. Tel: (762) 622 5073. Regular bus services from Mexico City and Acapulco.

Teotihuacán

Teotihuacán was the first known urban civilisation in Mesoamerica (*see pp8–9*), which, by the 4th century AD, had become the greatest power in the area. The most significant phase of development began in the 2nd century BC. By the 1st century AD, massive pyramids and temples testified to its importance as a religious and political centre. The second phase (c.AD 200–350) was one of conquest and continued development. In its final phase (c.AD 350–450) it reached its greatest splendour, occupying an area of some 20sq km (7¾ sq miles), with a

Spratling Museum. Porfirio Delgado & El Arco. Tel: (762) 622 1670. Open: Tue–Sat 9am–6pm, Sun 9am–3pm. Admission charge.

population estimated at 200,000. However, when the Aztecs arrived in the Valley of Mexico in the 12th century, the settlement had been abandoned for 700 years. Today, art and architecture offer the only clues to Teotihuacán's way of life.

Open: daily 7am–6pm. Son et Lumière Oct–Mar (7pm in English).

Veracruz

Mexico's principal seaport is also its oldest. It was here, on Good Friday in 1519, that Hernán Cortés arrived on the first stage of the Spanish Conquest. A replica of his ship *Marigallante* is on show in the harbour. He planted a cross (for which the settlement was named the True Cross), and the place became an important trading port with Europe.

Veracruz is one of the liveliest towns in Mexico, with an interesting mix of Mexican and Afro-Caribbean people. The main square, the Plaza de las Armas, is the scene of strolling musicians and never-ending activity.

The town is famous for its *jarocho* music and colourful Shrovetide Carnival. A recently added attraction is the new giant **Acuario** (Aquarium), impressive in both size and content, open all year round. The *malecón* (waterfront promenade) offers a pleasant walk along the busy harbour. Across the bay is the 16th-century island fortress of **San Juan de Ulúa**. It now houses a small regional museum.

South of town, Boca del Río has excellent open-air seafood restaurants. Lake Mandinga, beyond, offers boat trips through the mangroves.

427km (265 miles) east of Mexico City. Tourist office: Palacio Municipal. Tel: (229) 989 8817. www.veracruzturismo.com.mx. Flights from Mexico City. Bus and rail services.

Acuario Blvd Avila Camacho & Playon de Hornos. Open: daily, all year round 10am–7pm. **San Juan de Ulúa** Open: Tue–Sun 9am–4.30pm. Admission charge (Sun free).

Taxco offers a delightful study of the architecture of the region

Tour: To the Silver City

This is another popular tour from Mexico City, taking in flower-decked Cuernavaca, the stunningly pretty 'Silver City' of Taxco and the attractive spa resort of Ixtapan de la Sal, with wonderful mountain scenery thrown in.

Allow a full day.

From Mexico City, start from Reforma and take Insurgentes Sur south. Continue on toll highway 95 to Cuernavaca. This is a very pleasant route over the Ajusco Mountains, climbing up to a higher altitude before descending to Cuernavaca.

1 Cuernavaca

With its pleasant climate, Cuernavaca has long been a favourite weekend retreat for residents of Mexico City. Now that it is practically a suburb of the capital, with an increasing number of Mexicans (and foreigners) making it their permanent base, the town is often choked with traffic. Known affectionately as the City of Eternal Spring for its agreeable climate, Cuernavaca has a dazzling array of flowers.

The main square is charming, with plenty of flowers and greenery, the usual benches and a bandstand in the centre. On one side stands the elegant Governor's Palace. Opposite is a huge statue of Father Hidalgo's successor, José María Morelos, one of the heroes of the War of Independence against Spain. Alongside is the **Cuauhnáhuac Museum**, formerly the Palace of Cortés. Here you can see a Diego

Cuauhnáhuac Museum Leyva 100. *Tel: (777) 312 8171.* Open: Tue–Sun 9am–6pm. Admission charge.
Jardín Borda *Tel: (777) 318 8250.* Open: Tue–Sun 10am–5.30pm. Admission charge.

Rivera mural depicting the Conquest of Mexico, along with many other paintings and sculptures.

A short walk leads to the cathedral. This fortress-like structure, a former Franciscan church built in the 16th century, is set in an enclosed garden with chapels on either side. Its exterior could benefit from renovation, but the interior is a harmonious combination of original and modern elements. The cathedral is known for its *mariachi* Mass on Sundays.

Just beyond is the attractive **Jardín Borda**, with magnificent trees, fountains and a small boating lake, visited by Habsburg Emperor Maximilian and his wife Carlotta. If time permits, take a look at the Teopanzolco pyramid located near the railway station.
Continue on the R95 south to Taxco.

2 Taxco

With its red-roofed colonial-style houses clinging to the mountainside, Taxco (*see p72*) always makes a delightful impression. This is one of Mexico's most fascinating towns and it is a pleasure to wander about the tiny cobblestone streets as they wind their way steeply up the hillside.

Mexico's 'Silver City' prospered as a result of rich silver deposits mined in

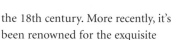

Woven rainbows make a warm souvenir of sunny days in Cuernavaca

the 18th century. More recently, it's been renowned for the exquisite silverware crafted here.

The city's focal point is the pretty little tree-shaded main square, but its jewel is the **Church of Santa Prisca**, built of local pinkish stone.
Rejoin the R95. Take the R55 northwest to Ixtapan de la Sal.

3 Ixtapan de la Sal

Ixtapan de la Sal is a spa resort, with cool green lawns, flowers and fountains surrounded by forestland. There is a municipal spa and, on the outskirts, a privately run park with the full range of facilities. Luxurious hotels have pools and thermal baths in Greco-Roman style.
Continue on the R55 to Toluca, and take the R15 back to Mexico City.

Santa Prisca Church Plaza Borda. Open: Mon–Sat 7am–8pm, Sun 6am–9pm.

The Pacific coast

Mexico's Pacific coastline stretches over 7,000km (4,350 miles), from the north where it meets California, down to its southern border with Guatemala. The slopes and valleys of the great Sierra Madre Occidental, which parallels the west coast, provide a lush green backdrop to much of the coastal scenery. In the southern regions there are large, thriving plantations of bananas, mangoes and coconuts. The whole coast is punctuated with beautiful bays ringed by mountains, and long stretches of sandy beaches broken up by rock formations.

Wooded hills meet curving Mismaloya Beach in Puerto Vallarta, Jaliscoa

The long, sandy beach at Ixtapa

Until the 1920s, the coast supported only a handful of small towns and tiny, isolated fishing villages. But, as more roads were built, tourism became possible. Starting with Acapulco, which has long been internationally famous, other resorts followed. Puerto Vallarta, further up the coast, grew rapidly to become Acapulco's rival in the popularity stakes. The stretch down to Manzanillo, labelled the Costa de Oro (Gold Coast), is also attracting a number of new resort hotels. Further north and into the Gulf of California are older-established resorts such as Mazatlán, Guaymas and Bahía Kino, which have drawn North American visitors for decades with their fine fishing and sailing.

The development of tourism was given a boost in the 1970s, when the government set up a trust fund known as FONATUR. With properly planned development, tourist centres like Ixtapa sprang up. Another project was the development of the Bahías de Huatulco, an extensive area of nine bays along Oaxaca's southern coastline.

Golden sands with year-round swimming in transparent seas, set against a hinterland that is exotic, mysterious and sometimes awe-inspiring, beckon visitors to feast on the many delights of Mexico's west coast – still pristine over much of its length, and with the luxury of space not easily found in other resort destinations. (*See map on pp50–51.*)

Acapulco

For many years the 'Pearl of the Pacific' reigned supreme as Mexico's number-one resort. Now, as new resorts have developed, Acapulco's glamorous reputation as a playground for the jet set has receded somewhat. Nevertheless, Acapulco still has the name, and this, coupled with its spectacular setting, assures its continuing place in the top league of popular tourist resorts.

Whatever your taste, Acapulco offers an excellent climate and lively atmosphere, day and night, in a stunning setting. The first sight of Acapulco Bay from the coastal road above it wins over most people. With the gorgeous sweep of its palm-fringed beach, high-rise hotels and backdrop of mountains, it is indeed spectacular. At night it becomes unforgettable, with hundreds of twinkling lights curving round the bay.

In its earlier days, Acapulco's western beaches and rocky coves drew the resort crowds. Popular beaches like Caleta and Caletilla were left to the locals as glitzy new hotels sprang up further along the bay. These days, tourist interest has shifted to Condesa and Los Hornos beaches, near the city's top-rated hotels. The beaches are always lively, with a wide range of aquatic activities such as parasailing, waterskiing and sailing.

The Acapulco lifestyle is seductive. Pollution problems in the bay discourage many people from swimming in the sea, so visitors tend to spend the day sipping large drinks from the comfort of their poolside sunloungers. The water is deliciously warm, and pools are attractively designed, usually set in tropical gardens right by the sea. Nevertheless, it is worth getting away from your hotel's watery idyll to take in a few experiences.

No visitor to Acapulco will want to miss the famous cliff divers of La Quebrada (*see pp80–81*), whose midday and evening performances are positively breathtaking. Or the Flying Men of Papantla who perform at the Acapulco Centre. On a glass-bottom boat trip to Isla Roqueta, you can see beautiful, multicoloured fish and marine plants as well as an image of the Virgin of Guadalupe submerged under a crystal-clear sea. Day or evening fiesta yacht cruises around the fine harbour offer live music and dancing, in addition to an overall view of the city that is unmatched from the land.

Night-time here is spectacular. The tropical air exudes an infectious excitement. The classic way to greet the evening is to watch one of Acapulco's technicolour sunsets. The best place to view the setting sun is Pie de la Cuesta, a few kilometres north of the town. Here, where the mountains meet the coastal plain of Coyuca Lagoon, you can stretch out in a hammock, gaze at the enormous waves crashing heavily on the long beach and enjoy a vividly hued sunset that seems to envelop the whole sky.

Afterwards, the social life is usually connected with hotel bars, before people drift off for dinner. Acapulco is teeming with eating places, from elegant hotel restaurants with icy air-conditioning, to open-air establishments in the hills, offering glittering views of the bay. For some, the only fitting ending to the day is dancing the night away at one of the many deafening discos, which are an essential part of fashionable Acapulco.

Bravo Town

This is a new ecotourism adventure park for the whole family, and includes white-water rafting opportunities for ages seven and up.
Free tel: (01 800) 514 6835.

Centro Internacional Para Convivencia Infantil (CICI)

Large theme park for children, with water slides, pools and dolphin shows.
Costera Miguel Alemán, by Playa Icasos.
Open: daily 10am–6pm.
Admission charge.

Fuerte de San Diego (Fort St James)

A museum containing exhibits dating back to the founding of Acapulco is housed inside this fort, which was built between 1615 and 1617 to defend the port against marauding pirates.
Calle Morelos and Playa Hornitos.
Tel: (744) 482 3828. Open: Tue–Sun 10.30am–5pm. Admission charge.

Papagayo Park

Many attractions for children, including an aviary, go-kart racing, roller-skating rink and boating on a small man-made lake.
Across from Playa Hornitos.
Tel: (744) 485 9623. Open: daily 8am–8pm. Free admission.
407km (253 miles) south of Mexico City. Information office: Costera Miguel Alemán 187. Frequent flights from Mexico City (45 minutes), other Mexican destinations and the US. Regular buses from Mexico City (about 5 hours).

The shimmering blue sea of Acapulco Bay is the perfect foil for dazzling white hotels

High fliers

Acapulco offers two very different types of spectacle, each involving daring feats that could justly be described as death-defying.

The story of Acapulco's celebrated cliff divers goes back to the early 1930s, when young boys would dive off the cliffs of La Quebrada for mere sport. With the arrival of tourism, the free show caught on, and today it is one of Acapulco's main attractions, rarely missed by any visitor. Athletic young men, perched on a sheer cliff over 40m (131ft) above the sea, make a daring swallow dive into a narrow cove, calculating their timing to the split second so as to enter the water on the swell. By day, the performances inspire admiration; by night, they can literally take your breath away. Tension builds as the diver clambers up the rock face, prays

Totonac Indians in El Tajín, 'flying' and dancing; these daring entertainers thrill the crowds

before the chapel on top and stands ready. At his given signal, flares are lit and down he goes! Everyone holds their breath until he reappears, seconds later, to loud acclaim. Spectators can view performances from the El Mirador Hotel and various public areas around.

High diving into water is one thing, on to dry land quite another – especially as performed by the Flying Men of Papantla. Several evenings a week at the Acapulco Centre, this ancient Totonac ritual – believed to relate to the rain gods and the vanilla harvest – is re-enacted in all its drama and genuine danger. Five Indian men in colourful attire climb up a 30m (98ft) high pole to stand on a tiny platform. Once ready, four of them suddenly cast off into space and spiral downwards around the pole, twirling on the end of ropes attached to their feet, in 13 rotations. The fifth man stays atop the platform playing a flute and beating a drum.

The participants are carefully selected young men, natives of Papantla, Veracruz, where the ritual originated. The dance is still performed in its native town, but for some years has been presented in various locales as a tourist attraction.

Cliff diving in Acapulco

Huatulco beach, shaded by thatched umbrellas, invites a carefree stroll on the sand

Bahías de Huatulco

Huatulco, developed by FONATUR (the government agency set up in the 1970s to develop new tourist resorts with a proper infrastructure), started in 1982. Located on Mexico's southern Pacific coast, the area marked for development covers nine bays and a tropical hinterland backed by the Sierra Madre.

Centred on Tangolunda Bay are several top-class hotels on the beachfront, with swimming pools and lush tropical landscaping. There are 36 beaches in the area. About 10 minutes away is the new inland town of La Crucecita, built in typical Mexican style with a main square and a bandstand. Boats depart from the marina at Santa Cruz (and several beachside hotels) for trips to other bays, some of which offer good swimming, snorkelling, wind-surfing, scuba diving and waterskiing. *291km (181 miles) south of Oaxaca. Information office: Paseo B Juárez s/n,*

Tangolunda Bay. Tel: (958) 581 0177. Flights from Mexico City, Oaxaca and other domestic destinations. Buses from Oaxaca and Acapulco.

Ixtapa-Zihuatanejo

Although they are totally separate, the two resorts are served by the same airport and tend to be listed together. Another product of FONATUR's planning, Ixtapa is now a fully fledged modern resort, complementing the fishing-village character of neighbouring Zihuatanejo.

Ixtapa

Until the early 1970s, Ixtapa was an isolated bay surrounded by dense virgin jungle. It has now developed into a sizeable resort with a string of modern hotels along a wide sandy beach, much favoured by Mexican families. Hotels offer a good selection of restaurants, and there are plenty of discos. One can take part in all the popular watersports here: waterskiing, scuba diving, snorkelling, windsurfing, parasailing and fishing. It has an 18-hole Robert Trent Jones course, and there is tennis and riding.

Zihuatanejo

About 7km (4¹/₃ miles) away, the old fishing village of Zihuatanejo lies in a lovely bay formed by the convergence of jungle and mountains. Although it has seen some changes in recent years, its rustic charm, fun restaurants and offbeat ambience provide a pleasing contrast to its modern neighbour, Ixtapa. The sheltered bay provides good swimming from several beaches. Small hotels amid the foliage lead down to Playa la Ropa, one of the most popular beaches. A very enjoyable boat trip crosses the bay to the beach of Playa las Gatas. The waters in this protected little cove offer wonderful snorkelling and diving. Open-air restaurants line the beach, which is popular with local families at weekends.

636km (395 miles) southwest of Mexico City. Municipal Tourist Office, Palacio Municipal. Tel: (755) 554 2001. Email: turismo@ixtapa-zihuatanejo.gob.mx. Flights from Mexico City, other Mexican destinations and the US. Bus service from Mexico City.

The Pacific coast

Fishing boats rest between outings on Zihuatanejo's Municipal Beach

Manzanillo and the Costa de Oro

With its ample bay, Manzanillo has long served as an important seaport. Local Indians are thought to have had contact with Chinese traders as far back as the 12th century, and it was from here that the Spanish set off for the Philippines and other lands. Cortés favoured it enough to spend part of his retirement here.

Manzanillo

Nowadays, Manzanillo is a major shipping port, with a rail link running inland. Fishermen know it as a great shellfish centre. For the visitor, however, the main focus of interest is the surrounding area.

It was the construction of **Las Hadas** (The Fairies) – a recreation centre resembling a Moorish fantasy, dreamt up by a Bolivian tin magnate as a haven for the jet set – that put Manzanillo on the map. Internationally famous (and the exotic location of the film *10*), this spectacular Arabian Nights-style complex of dazzling white houses, turrets and brilliantly coloured tropical flowers lies on the southern slopes of the Santiago Peninsula, where other fine hotels are also located.

The surrounding hills are covered by flats and villas, and development continues at a rapid pace.
349km (217 miles) from Guadalajara. Information office: Blvd Miguel de la Madrid 4960. Tel: (314) 333 2264.

Small fishing vessels lie at anchor in the historic harbour of Manzanillo

The rustic charm of the beach at Puerto Escondido

www.mazanillo.com.mx
Direct flights from Mexico City and other
Mexican destinations. Bus from Puerto
Vallarta (5 hours).
Las Hadas tel: (314) 331 0100.

Costa de Oro

From Manzanillo north to Puerto
Vallarta lies 286km (178 miles) of
long, sandy beaches and rocky coves
backed by verdant jungle. As with other
coastlines, it has acquired a name: the
Costa de Oro (Gold Coast). Highway
200 veers inland here, with turn-offs to
hotels and resorts, which are more
easily reached by bus transfers from
the airports of Manzanillo and
Puerto Vallarta.

Barra de Navidad

The sleepy character of this small
fishing village has been awakened by
the nearby Pueblo Nuevo tourism
complex and the Isla Navidad
development, featuring new hotels, a
marina and a golf course.
56km (35 miles) north of Manzanillo.

Costa de Careyes (Turtle Coast)

White beaches, palm trees and azure
lagoons backed by tropical vegetation
make up this region. The picturesque
Bel-Air Costa Careyes resort is an
attractive feature of this particularly
beautiful stretch of coastline.
20km (12½ miles) north of Tenacatita.

Melaque

Melaque's several small, sandy beaches
are surrounded by hills. A long-time
favourite with Mexicans and
Americans, the resort has plenty of
hotels, bars and restaurants.
11km (6¾ miles) north of Barra
de Navidad.

Tenacatita

This is the location of a self-contained
resort hotel with the delightful name
of the Blue Bay Village Los Angeles
Locos (The Crazy Angels), and it is
built around Tenacatita Bay. Visitors
can swim, fish and enjoy the air of
tranquillity.
19km (11¾ miles) north of Melaque.

Mazatlán

The largest commercial port on Mexico's Pacific coast, Mazatlán is also a thriving fishing centre. Its two, large, island-dotted bays, extensive beaches and 16km (10-mile) long seaside promenade make it a favourite resort for the northern population of the country. Situated directly across from the tip of the Baja Peninsula, there are daily ferries from here to La Paz and Cabo San Lucas. Large ocean liners also include Mazatlán in their itinerary.

Mazatlán is a big sport-fishing centre (marlin and sailfish tournaments are held here) and all necessary equipment can be hired. There are facilities for all other watersports, such as sailing, parasailing, waterskiing and scuba diving as well. Swimmers must take care, as the waves can be very rough in certain parts. Surfers head for the Playa Las Olas (Beach of High Waves) and some of the beaches north of town. For landlubbers there's golf, tennis, horse riding and plenty of welcoming resorts and hotels.

The centre of town is lively, with many bars and restaurants frequented by the younger set. The area around Plazuela Machado offers a small-town quiet ambience. Most restaurants in town serve fresh shrimp in abundance, prepared in many different ways. The shrimp industry here is the largest in Mexico; in fact, 80 per cent of its production is exported to the rest of North America. The region is also the world's second-largest producer of mangoes. A fine way of exploring is with the *pulmonias*, curious open-air taxis that puff their way up steep hills to offer visitors several panoramic hilltop views over the bays.

One of the best experiences while in Mazatlán is hiking and kayaking through the forests and lagoons of the Sierra Madre Occidental mountains which run parallel to the coast directly east of Mazatlán. The area is in the Pacific migratory flyway, and there are many special bird habitats documented by expert North American birdwatchers.

For mountain hiking, birdwatching tours and memorable kayak adventures through mangroves and secluded coves, contact: Mazatleco Nature Tours, Chihuaua 629, Fco. Villa. Tel. (669) 940 8687. www.mazatleco.com

Acuario Mazatlán

This modern, hexagonal aquarium features a shark tank and over 250 species of marine life, as well as a museum, a botanical garden and crocodile yard, plus a sea-lion show.

111 Avenida de los Deportes, near Avenida del Mar. Tel: (669) 981 7815. Open: daily 9am–6pm. Admission charge. Mazatlán is 505km (314 miles) northwest of Guadalajara. Information office: Coordinación General de Turismo de Sinaloa, Carnaval 1317, Mazatlán. Tel: (669) 981 8886. www.sinaloa-travel.com. Flights from Mexico City, other Mexican destinations and the US. Buses from Tijuana and Mexico City.

Puerto Ángel

This old fishing village, once a prominent seaport, is tucked away in a small turquoise bay on Oaxaca's southern coast. Progress has largely passed it by, and the place is for low-budget travellers looking for an outdoor life in casual surroundings. Most visitors head for the nearby beaches of Panteón or Zipolite, a particular favourite. Located 6km (3³/4 miles) west of town, it offers good swimming and surfing.

83km (52 miles) southeast of Puerto Escondido on Road 200. Daily bus from Oaxaca.

Puerto Escondido

Northwest of Puerto Ángel is Puerto Escondido (Hidden Port), which lies in a bay flanked by hills covered with exotic vegetation. There are over 90 hotels to choose from, yet it still retains a rustic charm. The village centre has now been closed to traffic and turned into a shopping and tourist area.

Along the beach are cafés and restaurants. Away from the centre, other good beaches include the popular Puerto Angelito, a rocky little cove with hammocks and various restaurants. Surfing is a big attraction in and around Puerto Escondido. To the east is Zicatela beach, renowned for its gigantic waves and strong undertow. Top-class surfing champions come here for competitions, as the waves are rated third best in the world.

264km (164 miles) south of Oaxaca. Flights from Mexico City. Buses from Oaxaca.

The peace and quiet at Puerto Ángel seem heaven-sent to stressed-out holidaymakers

Puerto Vallarta

Situated in the centre of the wide Bahía de (Bay of) Banderas, Puerto Vallarta is surrounded by cliffs and mountains covered by dense jungle. Until the early 1960s, it was a remote fishing village that rarely featured even on road maps. Then Night of the Iguana *was filmed on nearby Punta Mismaloya. Its stars, Richard Burton and Elizabeth Taylor, bought property in the hills. The village began to acquire a certain mystique. Today, with its superb beaches, it is one of Mexico's most popular resorts, whose casual ambience appeals to a younger, more bohemian type of clientele than does Acapulco.*

The old town still retains much of its original Mexican flavour, with narrow cobbled streets leading up into the hills. This downtown area bustles with shops, bars and tourists. Strung along the coast towards the airport are most of the resort's de luxe hotels, where fine beaches and tempting pools in tropical gardens provide good swimming. Puerto Vallarta is known for its lively nightlife, with no shortage of discos. The Cuale River, which runs through the town, divides to form the Isla del Río Cuale. This has shops, restaurants and an exotic view of the river against the backdrop of lush green mountains.

The Marina Vallarta offers luxury accommodation, golf and tennis, a commercial centre, and slips for some 300 boats. Fishermen still go out in the small hours to provide what is one of the staple foods for local families. A favourite beach is the Playa de los Muertos, which has excellent swimming and every variety of watersport, from parasailing and waterskiing to deep-sea fishing. Donkey polo and horse riding along the shore are also popular pastimes. Thatch-roofed restaurants and bars further enliven the scene.

One of the most popular excursions out of Puerto Vallarta is the boat trip to the wild jungle beach of Yelapa across Banderas Bay (*see p90*). Other boat trips take you to the beaches at Las Ánimas, Piedra Blanca and Mismaloya. Regular excursions explore the jungle hinterland, by vehicle or on horseback.

Some 12km (7½ miles) north of town is Nuevo Vallarta, which is a new resort built on a landscape of attractive estuaries and intricate canals. It offers luxurious hotels and a shopping centre, as well as a large marina.

The road continues to the small resort of Bucerías, and then follows the curve of the bay to some lovely isolated beaches including those of Cruz de Huanacaxtla, Arena Blanca and Destiladeras.

327km (203 miles) west of Guadalajara.

Information office: Plaza Marina Vallarta, 144.
Tel: (322) 221 2676/2680.
Flights from Mexico City, other Mexican destinations and the US.

Heavily wooded hills overlook the tidy beach of Playa Mismaloya in Puerto Vallarta

Boat trip: Puerto Vallarta to Yelapa

This is a popular excursion across the Bahía de Banderas to the jungle beach of Yelapa, with a short hike through the vegetation to a waterfall.

Allow a full day.

Go to the Terminal Marítima (Marina) about 8.30am and make your selection. The largest boat is the Sarape. One beer is included in the price, but no lunch. The boat sets off about 9am.

1 Puerto Vallarta's coastline

The *Sarape* has three decks, with good viewing from the top deck. The first part of the journey takes you slowly by the resort's long shoreline, with hotels standing out against the densely wooded mountains. After a while you will see the church tower, with its open-work crown, rising above the village. *Gradually the hotels and condominiums thin out, and the terrain becomes more rugged. About one and a half hours later you will pass by Mismaloya Beach and Los Arcos.*

2 Mismaloya

The beach still lives on its reputation as the setting for the film *Night of the Iguana* (you will doubtless be reminded of this fact). Beachside food and drink stalls are plentiful, and the warm waters and exotic marine plants invite exploration on another occasion. In front, several giant boulders rise from the sea to form natural arches – hence their name, Los Arcos. They are home to a bird colony and are also a popular area for snorkelling.

The boat continues along the tropical coastline until you spy the distant beach of Yelapa, tucked away at the foot of jungle-covered mountains. A small boat then ferries passengers to the nearby jetty.

3 Yelapa

The setting is magnificent, with a backdrop of tropical mountains towering around you. The beach is littered with open-air restaurants and vendors. There is plenty of activity at the bay, with swimming, waterskiing and speedboats whizzing around. You can settle down to an informal lunch on arrival, or proceed with the waterfall excursion. Eager boatmen await your custom on the beach. Fix a price before accepting. The boat ride takes approximately five minutes across to the tiny Indian village of Yelapa.

4 Through the jungle

After a somewhat undignified exit from the boat, you arrive in tiny Yelapa village; curious children, stray dogs and washing lines make an unexpected contrast to TV satellite dishes. Someone will lead you on the route, which goes up rough steps and over large boulders to enter the jungle proper, with its palms and lush tropical vegetation. The walk takes about 20 minutes.

Passing by a river bed far below, used by the local women for washing, you will come to **La Cascada el Bosque**. Just beyond is the waterfall. In a dramatic setting, with huge boulders amid the encroaching jungle, it cascades over steep rocks to a pool which, during and after the rainy season, is quite full and tempting enough to swim in. By the end of the dry season, however, the fall can be reduced to a mere trickle, and the pool reflects an unappealing copper colour. *Return to the edge of the bay, where a boat will soon arrive to take you back to Yelapa beach. At about 2pm a signalling hoot will be heard from the Sarape for departure at 2.50pm, to arrive in Puerto Vallarta at 5pm.*

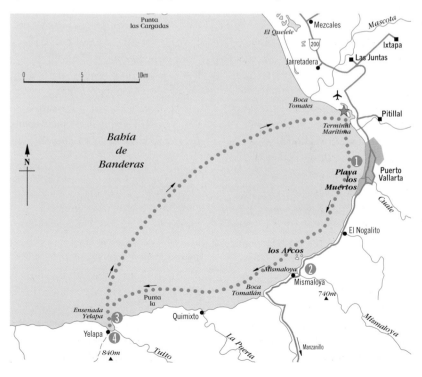

Southeastern Mexico and the Yucatán

This giant landmass, which completes Mexico's horn shape, encompasses the states of Chiapas, Tabasco, Campeche, Yucatán and Quintana Roo. It is bounded on the north by the Gulf of Mexico and on the south by the Pacific. To the east is the Caribbean, while to the southeast it shares a border with Guatemala and Belize.

The range of attractions within this region is enormous, from ancient ruins, Indian villages and colonial towns to modern beach resorts, and a striking diversity of landscapes. In Chiapas, steamy jungles contrast with cloud-

Southeastern Mexico and the Yucatán

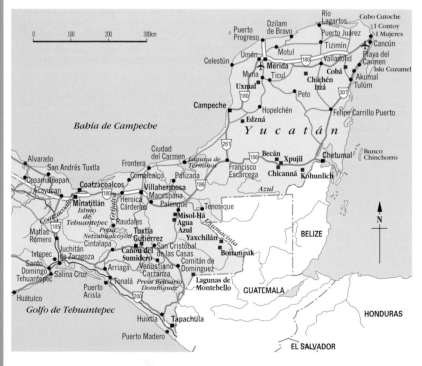

The Mayan city of Chichén Itzá, deep in the jungle

covered mountains, where temperatures can be cool. The state offers some stunning scenery, with lakes and waterfalls, rivers and a dramatic canyon, in addition to a wealth of flora and fauna, and a fascinating look at the life of indigenous peoples.

Campeche is characterised by rolling hills and tropical rainforests, while the Yucatán is a flat limestone shelf covered by low scrubland, with underground rivers, caves and *cenotes* (natural sinkholes). Quintana Roo is largely a wilderness of jungle, swamps and lakes. However, the development of popular Cancún and other beach resorts down its eastern Caribbean coast has put it

firmly on the map. Perhaps the biggest attraction is the wealth of archaeological sites scattered throughout the area. This region was the home of the Maya, whose magnificent cities bear testimony to a great past. Its major ruins are easily reached: Palenque, set deep in the jungle; Chichén Itzá, the most famous and best restored of the Yucatán's Mayan ruins; and splendid Uxmal, acclaimed as one of the best examples of Classic Mayan architecture. Mexico has 21 sites designated by UNESCO as World Heritage Sites, which ranks it first in the Americas and fifth in the world.

Cancún

In a very real sense, Cancún is the child of a silicon chip! The Mexican government used a computer to select an ideal location for a brand-new resort, and it came up with Cancún, a strip of virgin sand and deserted jungle on the coast of Quintana Roo. This was the first project of FONATUR (see p77). Included in the concept was the provision of local employment, and a boost to the region's economy.

Cancún has proved a success story. Begun in 1974, it has grown into one of Mexico's most popular resorts, thanks to powdery white beaches, clear turquoise waters and all-encompassing facilities. Its proximity to Florida makes it a convenient spot for travellers from Europe and the east coast of America.

Another point in Cancún's favour is its pleasant year-round climate, as cool sea breezes prevent it from getting overly hot during the summer months. Do be aware, however, that in autumn this coastline can be subject to strong winds and very unsettled weather, including hurricanes.

The resort is divided into two areas. Downtown Cancún is made up of chic shopping malls with stores and boutiques, restaurants and discos. There are also handicraft centres, but prices are often higher here than elsewhere in Mexico, because everything is brought in from outside.

Quite separate to the town is the Zona Hotelera (Hotel Zone), which extends along 19km (12 miles) of sandbar, with the Caribbean on one side and a lagoon on the other. Two thin strips of land, north and south, connect it to the mainland. Hotels are plentiful and come in an assortment of categories and shapes (architects have had a field day here). The sand is soft white powder, remaining cool enough to walk on, and the turquoise shades of the Caribbean are unbeatable. Greenery and coconut palms offer idyllic swimming conditions in certain parts. The best and safest beaches are those on the Bay of Isla Mujeres. Around the eastern end of the peninsula, a strong undertow and heavy surf can make swimming very dangerous. Always look for the red flag warnings on beaches.

A wide variety of aquatic sports can be enjoyed here: windsurfing, jet-skiing and parasailing are very popular. Motor boats and sailing boats, Hobie cats, canoes and kayaks are all available for hire. There is sailing, deep-sea fishing, diving and snorkelling; good areas are around the reefs between Cancún and Isla Mujeres. Equipment can be hired from the major hotels or marinas. There is also golf at the 18-hole Pok-Ta-Pok Robert Trent Course, and tennis at the courts adjoining some hotels. Many evenings offer spectacular sunsets, while at night the pace is fast and furious, with an abundance of discos and nightspots to choose from.

Numerous one-day excursions include daily trips to the islands of Isla Mujeres and Cozumel (*see pp96–7*), cruises on the Nichupte Lagoon for snorkelling, and night cruises. Glass-bottomed boats are ideal for viewing the rich underwater marine life, while a visit to the bird sanctuary on Isla Contoy (*see p142*) is another option. Don't miss a trip down the so-called Mayan Riviera, to the Mayan ruins at Tulúm (*see p109*), with stop-offs at some of the beautiful lagoons and bays on the way, including the Sian Ka'an Biosphere Reserve (*see p142*).
321km (199 miles) east of Mérida, on the northeastern tip of the Yucatán Peninsula.
Information office: Avenida Cobá, corner Avenida Nader. Open: Mon–Fri 9am–2pm and 4–7pm. Tel: (998) 884 6531. www. gocancun.com. Regular domestic and international flights. Also charters from the US and Europe. Buses from Mérida.

MAYAN RIVIERA

This coastal stretch runs for 160km (99 miles) south of Cancún. A well-kept two-lane motorway runs inland through scrub forests, with an increasing number of short turn-offs to beach resorts, lagoons, a marina development, theme park and a variety of attractions.

The Instituto Nacional de Arqueologia Historia (INAH) will help you to organise your archaeological sightseeing tours in the area.
Next to Cancún Centre, Blvd Kukulkan, Km 9.5. Tel: (998) 881 0400. Open: 9am–6pm. Alongside is the Museo Arqueologico de Cancún. Tel: (998) 883 0305. Open: Tue–Fri 9am–8pm, Sat & Sun 10am–7pm.

The stunning white beaches of Cancún

Akumal

Akumal lies in an idyllic Caribbean setting with small bungalows dotting a palm-fringed beach, and soft white sand curving around a sparkling bay. This is a well-known centre for snorkelling and skin-diving, offering expert instruction and ideal conditions.
101km (63 miles) south of Cancún.

Playa del Carmen

This has grown into a popular resort among younger people, with plenty of action along its long sandy beach, which is lined with hotels, bars and restaurants. Ferries operate from here to Cozumel.
66km (41 miles) south of Cancún.

Puerto Aventuras

The ambitious new development of Puerto Aventuras, further down the coast, caters to the affluent. It is attractively designed, with hotels, villas, apartments, shopping centres, restaurants and an 18-hole golf course. The deep-water marina can accommodate large luxury yachts.
97km (60 miles) south of Cancún.

Tulúm

119km (74 miles) south of Cancún.
See p109.

Xcaret

Now developed into a large 'Eco-Archaeological Park', Xcaret's attractions include underground swim-through subterranean caves, cavorting with dolphins, snorkelling, a tropical aquarium and butterfly pavilion, and spectacular evening shows. Small Mayan ruins also dot the place.
71km (44 miles) south of Cancún.
Between Playa del Carmen and Akumal.
Tel: (994) 871 5200. www.xcaret.com.
Open: daily, May–Nov 8.30am–10pm;
Dec–Apr 8.30am–9pm.
Admission charge.

Xel-Há

Aptly described as a 'natural aquarium', the Xel-Há national park consists of four interlocking lagoons in stunning shades of turquoise and blue. Swimming and snorkelling are permitted in its crystal-clear waters which abound with tropical fish. Equipment can be hired.
122km (76 miles) south of Cancún.
Between Akumal and Tulúm. Tel: (998)
884 9422. www.xel-ha.com. Open: daily
9am–6pm. Admission charge.

CARIBBEAN ISLANDS
Cozumel

Cozumel ('Island of Swallows' in Mayan), 53km (76 miles) long and 17km (10^{1}/2 miles) wide, is the larger of the two islands that lie off the northeast coast of the Yucatán Peninsula. With beautiful white sandy beaches, palm trees and turquoise waters, it offers all the relaxation of a desert-island hideaway. The principal town, San Miguel, has a lively main square.

The reefs around the island are a paradise for snorkelling and scuba diving. The most famous is the

Palancar Reef, about a mile (1.5km) offshore. Others include the reefs of San Francisco, Maracaíbo, Colombia, Santa Rosa Wall and Yaceb. Chancanab Lagoon, in the interior of the island, also offers excellent swimming and snorkelling amid tropical fish.

20km (12¹/₂ miles) from the mainland. Ferries from Playa del Carmen take about 1 hour 15 minutes. Connected by air with Mexico City and US destinations.

Isla Mujeres

The tiny island of Isla Mujeres (Island of Women) lies north of Cozumel. It measures only 8km by 1km (5 by ²/₃ miles) and can easily be explored on foot or by hired moped. Relaxed and informal, the island has a special appeal for the young and adventurous. There is snorkelling and scuba diving at the El Garrafón National Park, a coral reef just offshore with shoals of tropical fish. Los Manchones, on the southern end of the island, is another good spot.

10km (6¹/₄ miles) from the Yucatán mainland. There are regular ferries from Puerto Juárez and Punta Sam, which also carry cars.

The coral reef is close to shore on Isla Mujeres

Chichén Itzá

The old Mayan/Toltec city of Chichén Itzá is one of Mexico's great archaeological sites, and a highlight for any visitor to the Yucatán. The site extends over a large clearing in the jungle, and is considered one of the best-preserved pre-Columbian sites in the country.

Chichén means 'place of the well' in Mayan. The Itzá were a Mayan sect who occupied the original settlement, which dates back as early as AD 360. Although the city later fell into decline, it flourished again under the Toltecs, who arrived in the 10th century and added to many of the existing buildings. It reached its peak in the

A reclining *chacmool* figure on the Temple of the Warriors gazes across the site

THE DESCENT OF KUKULKÁN

The Mayas believed that their great sun god Kukulkán – also known as Quetzalcóatl, the plumed serpent – returned to earth at the spring and autumn equinoxes. This long-lost legend was rediscovered by an archaeologist who found that, on those days, the serrated shadow cast by the corner angle of El Castillo forms the body of a serpent gliding down the northwest stairway to the carved head of their revered god. The equinoxes occur on or around 21 March and 22 September, and each year vast crowds come from all over to witness this intriguing spectacle.

11th and 12th centuries, but was abandoned soon after.

The site is divided into the northern and southern groups. Start with the northern group (or 'new Chichén'), dominated by the magnificent El Castillo (The Castle), or Pyramid of Kukulkán. Each side has a stairway of 91 steps which, including the top platform, makes a total of 365. A handrail assists

Chichén Itzá

Site plan

1. Juego de Pelota
2. Temazcalli
3. Juego de Pelota
4. Columnata del Noroeste
5. Templo de las Mesas
6. Tzompantli
7. Casa de las Aguilas
8. Templo de los Jaguares
9. Edifico Sur
10. Templo Norte
11. Casa de los Metates
12. Templo de Venado
13. Chichán-chob (Casa Colorada)
14. Iglesia
15. Templo de los Tableros
16. Akab-Dzib

the climb to the top, which offers a magnificent view of the site. Down below, a small entrance leads up dark, narrow steps to two inner chambers, containing a red 'Jaguar Throne' with jade eyes, and a reclining *chacmool* sculptural figure.

The Templo de los Guerreros (Temple of the Warriors) is an impressive building of large columns and a *chacmool* altar. Below is the Grupo de las Mil Columnas (Group of a Thousand Columns), with carvings of plumed serpents. The Juego de Pelota (Ball Court) is the largest of its kind and has excellent acoustics.

A path into the jungle leads to the sinister Cenote de los Sacrificios (Sacred Well), where the skeletons of young girls were discovered, along with treasures of jade, gold and other artefacts.

Structures of major interest in the southern group (or 'old Chichán') include the reconstructed Tumba del Gran Sacerdote (Tomb of the High Priest); El Caracol (The Snail), an ancient observatory, with a spiral stair leading to the top, where the Maya studied the solar system and made astronomical calculations; the Edificio de las Monjas (Nunnery); Chichán-chob or Casa Colorada (Red House); and the Iglesia (Church). Son-et-lumière shows take place every evening except in bad weather.

120km (75 miles) east of Mérida. For information contact the Hotel Mayaland. Tel: (998) 887 2450. Open: daily 8am–6pm (summer), 8am–5.30pm (winter). Admission charge.
Most visitors take a tour from Mérida.

The Mayan world

The Spaniard Antonio de Herrera described what he saw in 'the Indies' about a hundred years after Cortés first landed in Mexico. The people he wrote of were the Maya, whose culture flourished between AD 300 and 900. They built their huge, stately pyramids all over Central America, from Yucatán to Honduras, without the use of the wheel, beasts of burden or any metal in their constructions. At their peak, they perfected the most complex writing system in the hemisphere, mastered the intricacies of mathematics and created an astrological calendar of amazing ingenuity and accuracy.

Their society was rigidly stratified: priest-nobles and warriors at the top, then a middle class of merchants, administrators, overseers and artisans. The lowest ranks were mainly slaves. Their gods and sub-gods were many and voracious, and ordered people's lives with bloodthirsty harshness. Appeasing them meant human torture and sacrifice, usually virgins thrown into the sacred *cenotes* (sinking wells) that are the Yucatán's only sources of fresh water.

Years of scholarship, painstaking excavation and careful analysis have produced a picture of what life might have been like before the Conquest. A typical family, of perhaps five to seven members, arose before dawn to a breakfast of hot chocolate or, if they were poor, a thick maize drink, *tamales*, or the flat maize pancakes called *tortillas*. Their one-room thatched house was made of poles woven together and covered with dried mud. Meals of corn, squash, beans and the occasional rabbit or turkey were prepared by the women, who also wove. The men worked in the fields, or built temples and

Detail of a Mayan plate painting

The Mayan city of Becan dates from AD 600–1000

pyramids. At the end of the day, the family would chant and pray, and perform a ritual bloodletting – their central act of piety.

High points in the year centred on attending royal marriages, ceremonies related to the calendar, the sacrifice of a captive or a loser of the Ball Game. They beautified themselves by filing their teeth and inlaying them with round chips of jade or pyrite. The sloping foreheads and flattened heads they so admired were achieved by strapping boards round the heads of their infants; parents encouraged the much-prized crossed eyes by hanging small beads over the noses of their children. Young men, it is thought, painted themselves black until marriage, and later engaged in ritual scarring and tattooing.

It is estimated that 1.2 million Mayans still live in the state of Chiapas, and nearly 5 million more are spread throughout the Yucatán, Belize, Guatemala, Honduras and El Salvador. The Mundo Maya project is trying to promote awareness of their culture, past and present, and encourage tourism that respects both the people and the environment.

MÉRIDA

Mérida is the capital of the Yucatán, and the main base for visiting Uxmal (*see pp110–11*) and Chichén Itzá (*see pp98–9*). Industrial growth has changed its formerly sleepy image, though it retains the elegant mansions and the graceful traditions of its people. Founded in 1542 on the ruins of a much older Indian city, its great wealth derived from *henequen* (a fibre product used to make rope). Today, local people are specially known for fine leatherwork, Panama hats and embroidered shirts.

Two of Mérida's most attractive features are its delightful *zócalo* and bustling daily market.
1,497km (930 miles) northeast of Mexico City. Information office: Teatro Peon Contreras, Calle 59. Tel: (999) 924 9290. www.merida.gob.mx
Flights from the US, Mexico City and other domestic destinations.

A typical scene in Mérida

Casa de Montejo

Now occupied by Banamex, the handsome 16th-century Montejo House is noted for its plateresque façade.
Calle 63, Plaza Principal. Open: Mon–Fri 9am–5pm, Sat 9am–2pm.

Catedral

This 16th-century cathedral with a fortress-like exterior is the largest in the Yucatán Peninsula, and the oldest on the American continent.
Plaza Principal. Open: Mon–Sat 6am– noon & 4–7pm, Sun 6am–1pm & 4–8pm.

Palacio Cantón

This houses the **Museo Regional de Antropología** and gives an insight into the Yucatán's history.
Calle 43, at Paseo de Montejo. Tel: (999) 923 0557. Open: Tue–Sat 8am–8pm, Sun 8am–2pm. Admission charge (Sun free).

Palacio del Gobierno

The elegant, late 19th-century Governor's Palace encloses a pretty patio, and the staircase walls are covered with murals illustrating symbolic and mythical themes.
Plaza Principal.

Palacio Municipal

The Town Hall, built in 1735, features arches and a clock tower.
Instituto Nacional de Antropología e Historia-Yucatán. Km 6.5, Antigua Carretera a Progreso. Tel: (999) 928 2020. Open Mon–Fri 9am–5pm

OTHER SIGHTS
Bonampak

These Mayan ruins deep in the jungle
of eastern Chiapas are not easy to
reach. Bonampak ('Painted Walls' in
Mayan) is famous for its frescoes
depicting warriors and battle scenes.
*130km (81 miles) southeast of Palenque.
Open: daily 8am–4.45pm. Charter
planes from Palenque, Tuxtla Gutiérrez,
San Cristóbal de las Casas or Comitán,
or by road in dry season.*

Sumidero Canyon and the Grijalva River

Cañon del Sumidero

Boat trips along the Grijalva River pass
beside the sheer walls of this stratified
canyon, giving a close-up view of the
wildlife (*see p136*). You can look down
into the canyon from several *miradores*
(viewpoints) on the road above.
*Chiapa de Corzo is 15km (9¹/2 miles) east
of Tuxtla.*

Cascadas Agua Azul

These jungle waterfalls present a
dazzling sight of cascades in shades
of turquoise that come tumbling over
limestone rocks (*see p136*). Some 42km
(26 miles) northeast, a left turn off the
road to Palenque leads to the delightful
little cascade of Misol-Há, a wonderful
spot for swimming.
*55km (34 miles) south of Palenque village.
Admission charge. Best by own vehicle or
by an organised excursion from Palenque.*

Lagunas de Montebello

These lakes, surrounded by mountains,
peaceful pine forests and wildlife, are
renowned for their different hues of
blue, green and violet (*see p136*).
*103km (64 miles) southeast of San
Cristóbal de las Casas. Free admission.
Buses from San Cristóbal via Comitán.*

Río Bec Group

An archaeological zone of several sites.
Most accessible are Chicanná, Becán
and Xpujil. Guides recommended for
visit to Calakmul, Balankú, Río Bec
itself and other sites in the area. Off
Highway 186 to Chetumal are the ruins
of Kohunlich in its exotic surroundings.
*Main zone: 120km (75 miles) west of
Chetumal. Admission charge for
some sites. Best by own vehicle or
organised tour.*

Yaxchilán

Set high on a loop of the Usumacinta
River in jungle inhabited by Lacandon
Indians, these Mayan ruins date back to
between AD 500 and 800 (*see p133*).
*32km (20 miles) east of Bonampak. Open:
daily 8am–4.45pm. Admission charge.*

Palenque

Some consider these Mayan ruins – once highly coloured – to be the most sensational in Mexico. Lying in the humid tropical growth of Chiapas, they seem steeped in brooding mystery, reminiscent of the 'Lost Cities' of bygone times. Palenque was occupied from about 300 BC to the end of the 8th century AD, when it was abandoned and slowly taken over by vegetation.

At the entrance are little stalls set up by local Lacandon Indians, recognisable by their long, straight, black hair and proud demeanour. Entering the site, you will pass two small ruined temples on the right before coming upon the most interesting building of all. The Templo de las Inscripciones (Temple of the Inscriptions) dates from the end of the 7th century. In 1949, down in the bowels of the temple, archaeologist Alberto Ruiz Lhuillier uncovered a hidden crypt containing the sarcophagus of chieftain Pakal, surrounded by treasures. This was the first time in Mexico that a tomb was found inside a temple. Recent explorations have unearthed other such tombs in the region.

An easy climb from the rear takes you to the top of the temple, which has magnificent carvings and glyphs of Mayan scenes. From here you can descend to the crypt and view the royal tomb. Be careful as lighting is poor and the stairway is slippery.

The grassy slopes of the site are scattered up and down with other buildings. Atop a large platform is the imposing *palacio* (palace), which was evidently occupied by dignitaries for special ceremonies. Delicate carvings also adorn these walls. Behind the palace on the right, across a shallow stream a short distance away, lies a curious little group of temples all with roof combs. Known as the Templo del Sol (Temple of the Sun), Templo de la Cruz (Cross) and Templo de la Cruz Foliada (Foliated Cross), they are all perched high up on grassy mounds.

The oldest excavated building is the Templo del Conde (Temple of the Count). The top of the adjacent Grupo Norte (Northern Group) gives a good view of the site. Beyond this is a small museum with clay figurines, jewels

Palenque

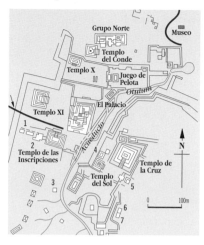

Site plan

1   Templo XII
2   Templo XIII
3   Casa del Jaguar
4   Edifico XIV
5   Templo de la Cruz Foliada
6   Templo XVIII
7   Templo XVIIIa

of jade, shell, mother-of-pearl and obsidian, and other artefacts.

The dense tropical vegetation in and around the site is magnificent. If you want to explore the interior, go with a guide and keep to the paths. The almost mystical harmony between these exotic surroundings and the ancient man-made splendours makes this a very special place (*see p133*). (Use insect repellent liberally.)

143km (89 miles) southeast of Villahermosa, near Palenque village. Information office: 3a Calle Ote. Norte S/N. Tel: (934) 50356. www.mesoweb.com/palenque. Open: daily 8am–5pm. Admission charge (Sun & holidays free). Most people take a day's excursion from Villahermosa. Bus services from Villahermosa and other towns, and flights from other parts of southern Mexico.

Palenque's Temples of the Cross, the Foliated Cross and the Sun (left to right)

The Chamulas

The highlands around San Cristóbal de las Casas are inhabited by about 65,000 people descended from two Maya groups, the Tzotzils and the Tzeltals. Although close geographically, each group speaks its own dialect, has its own traditions and preserves its distinctive customs.

The Tzotzil-speaking Chamulas live in the district of San Juán Chamula, not far from San Cristóbal. The tiny village focuses around a small mystical church which is the scene of spiritual practices with pre-Christian influences. The floor is strewn with pine needles and stuck with candles. Chamulas chant amid clouds of incense, while *curanderos* (healers) cure ailments, uttering incantations as they work with a rather surprising mixture of ingredients, including a chicken, eggs, *posh* (the local firewater), Pepsi Cola and a candle.

The Chamulas worship John the Baptist and some 40 other saints, whose statues are adorned with mirrors. Sometimes the statues are tied up and temporarily 'put in jail' as a punishment for not responding to solicitation! Visitors may enter the church after paying a nominal fee at the small office across the square. Note that photography within the church is strictly forbidden at all times.

The Sunday morning market, which takes place in front of the church, is the meeting place for Indians from all the surrounding villages. The Chamula men are usually dressed in white, while a black tunic signifies some position of

Chamula Indians in the plaza at Chamula

authority. The ruling elders, attired in special costumes, with ribboned hats and carrying staffs, sit outside the church and help sort out the villagers' problems. San Juan Chamula is also renowned for its numerous religious festivals, which combine pagan and Christian beliefs. These are organised by a selected major-domo, or chief steward, who must pay all costs, including food and drink. One of the liveliest festivals is the Carnival, just before Lent, when the participants wear masks, take part in races and run barefoot over live coals.

Traditional dress

Samples of weaving and traditional garments in San Cristóbal

SAN CRISTÓBAL DE LAS CASAS

This curious little town, set high among the cloud forests, is Spanish in style, with cobbled streets, coloured houses with tiled roofs and some fine churches. The place, which is small and easy to explore, seems still to belong to the 18th century. In recent years, though, increased tourism, and the huge influx of Chamulas expelled from their villages for converting to Evangelical Protestantism (a result of US missionaries at work), is gradually changing the place.

83km (52 miles) northeast of Tuxtla Gutiérrez. Information office: Palacio Municipal.

Tel: (967) 678 0665. Regular buses from Tuxtla Gutiérrez (about 2 hours).

Catedral

The main square, Plaza 31 de Marzo, is dominated by this large, early Baroque building. Started in 1547, it was substantially transformed in the 18th century. Beyond the stark façade the church contains gilded altars and two remarkable paintings: the *Virgin of Sorrows* to the left of the altar and *The Magdalena* inside the sacristy.

Central Marketplace

Beside the Santo Domingo church, a splendid assortment of fruit, vegetables, medicinal herbs, flowers and live poultry is sold daily by traders whose costumes denote their tribe (the ribbons on the Zinacantecos' hats indicate how many children they have). The liveliest market day is Saturday.

Na-Bolom (House of the Jaguar)

Founded by Danish archaeologist Frans Blom and his Swiss photographer wife Trudi (both deceased), who devoted years to studying and helping the Indians of the region, this institution now runs as a study centre (and guest-house), with small museums and an extensive library of books on the Maya.

Chamula crafts market in front of the church of Santo Domingo

Avenida Vicente Guerrero 33. Tel: (967)
678 1418. www.nabolom.org. Open for
tours only: Mon–Sun 11.30am
(Spanish), 4.30pm (English).
Admission charge.

Templo de Santo Domingo

St Dominic's Church is notable for its
impressive Baroque exterior, gilt
Rococo interior and carved gilt pulpit.
In front of the church, Chamula
women have established a mini-market
selling brightly coloured woven goods.
Santo Domingo, on the corner of Lázaro
Cárdenas and Nicaragua.

SAN JUAN CHAMULA

See pp106–7.

TULÚM

What it lacks in comparison with the
greats in terms of architectural merit,
Tulúm makes up for in terms of its
location. As the only sizeable Mayan
city found on the coast, its dramatic
setting on a cliff top overlooking the
Caribbean is an attraction in itself. The
stone fortifications that surround it
were a response to the constant wars in
the region.

Tulúm dates back to the 13th
century. In 1518, it was sighted by a
Spanish expedition led by Juan de
Grijalva which was passing by the coast.
The Spaniards were impressed by its
size and splendour, likening it to
Seville. Part of the old surrounding wall
remains today. The prominent **Castillo**
(Castle) commands a splendid view of

Visit Tulúm in the early morning, then retreat
to the beach when tour buses arrive later

the coral-dotted sea. Above the
entrance is a stucco sculpture of a
'descending god', an image that recurs
above the main doorways of the
Templo del Dios Descendente and the
Templo de los Frescos. Various
interpretations of what this figure
represents exist, including one theory
about earthly visitations by aliens!

Another place of archaeological
interest is **Cobá**, which lies 44km
(27 miles) to the northwest. Never
found by the Spaniards, this once great
ceremonial centre flourished from the
5th to the end of the 12th century. It
was the most important Mayan city in
its time, until Chichén Itzá rose to
power after AD 600. Its ruins spread
over a large area of humid jungle and
lakes, and can be reached by car, or by
organised excursion buses from
Cancún, which offer regular services.
Tulúm: 119km (74 miles) south of
Cancún. Can only be reached by car or
bus. Open: daily 7am–5pm. Cobá: open:
7am–6pm. Admission charge (Sun &
holidays free).

Uxmal

The famous archaeological site of Uxmal is perhaps the most elegant of all Mexico's Mayan ruins. Along with Chichén Itzá, it represents one of the Yucatán's major attractions. Smaller and more compact than Chichén, it contains some of the most beautiful examples of classic Mayan architecture. As Chichén Itzá developed, Uxmal's importance gradually waned until it lapsed into obscurity. Uxmal, which means 'thrice built', was probably founded in the 6th century AD. It became an important ceremonial centre and flourished between the 7th and 10th centuries. Its monuments, covered with delicate carvings, belong to the typical Puuc style of the Maya Classic period.

Soaring above you as you enter the site is the imposing Pirámide del Adivino (Pyramid of the Soothsayer). According to a curious legend, it was built in one night by a dwarf with the help of his mother, a witch. Four stairways lead steeply up the pyramid. With the help of a rope you can climb up two of the stairways to the temple at the top, which offers a magnificent view of the site and surrounding jungle. The route

Archaeologists have yet to decipher the original use of the 74-room Nuns' Quadrangle

leads through a classic pointed Mayan arch to the Cuadrángulo de las Monjas (Nuns' Quadrangle), so named by the Spaniards owing to its rows of cells and the delicacy of its carved façades. The structures, called simply the North, South, East and West Buildings, are arranged around a broad courtyard, and are noted for their symmetry and elegant proportions. Decorations and carvings of the rain god, Chac, appear on some of the outer walls.

From the Nuns' Quadrangle you will pass the small Juego de Pelota (Ball Court) and Casa de las Tortugas (House of Turtles) before arriving at the impressive Palacio del Gobernador (Governor's Palace), which stands on a massive platform. An architectural masterpiece, it is noted for its exquisite façade and the geometric decorations in the frieze. Other structures of note

Uxmal

Site plan

1 Juego de Pelota
2 Casa de las Tortugas
3 Palomar
4 Cuadrángulo de las Monjas
5 Templo de Cementario
6 Grupo de las Columnas
7 Grupo Noroeste
8 Grupo Oeste
9 Templo de los Ciempiés
10 Templo de los Falos

include the Gran Pirámide (Great Pyramid) and the Palomar (Dovecote). *76km (47 miles) south of Mérida. Open: daily 8am–5pm. Admission charge (Sun & holidays free). Son et lumière: every*

evening 7pm (Spanish), 9pm (English), weather permitting. Admission charge. Local bus service from Mérida or organised excursion.

Surrounding sites

South of Uxmal are several smaller Mayan sites worth visiting. About 21km (13 miles) southeast on the R261 are the ruins of **Kabah**. The most striking building is the one known as the Codz-Pop, which features some 250 masks of the rain god Chac. Codz-Pop ('rolled-up mat') refers to the odd, trunk-like noses of the masks. Across the road stands a solitary Mayan arch.

Further along the R261, a left turn leads to Sayil, Xlapak and Labná in the **Puuc Archaeological Zone**, whose style is characterised by plain walls with elaborate stucco and stone ornamentation above. **Sayil** is dominated by the splendid Palacio (Palace), embellished with *chac* masks, columns and a pair of reptiles flanking an upside-down figure. **Xlapak's** main building is a contrast of subtlety and splendid exuberance, including more long-nosed masks of the god Chac. **Labná** is known for its monumental arch, the most profusely decorated of all Mayan architecture.

Return to the R261, and continue south. At Hopelchén take the R180 to Campeche and turn left to **Edzná**. Most notable here is the Templo de los Cinco Pisos (Temple of Five Levels). *Open: daily 8am–5pm. Admission charge (Sun & holidays free).*

Villahermosa

Amid the steamy jungles and swamplands of Tabasco lies Villahermosa, the state capital. Important oil discoveries in the 1970s and agricultural development in the region transformed the place into a fast-growing boom town. This is macho country, with great strapping ranchers seen about town (a lone woman here may well find herself the object of too much attention).

While its modern, brash image may not appeal to some, the city offers some pleasant diversions. You can stroll about the busy pedestrianised area downtown and on to the Grijalva River, where the *malecón* (promenade) invites a meander along its banks. Music relayed through 'singing lamp-posts' adds a rather charming touch. Boat trips along the Grijalva provide a glimpse of typical Tabasco jungle terrain (the ride lasts about two hours, and lunch is served on board). For many tourists travelling by air, Villahermosa serves merely as an overnight stop before visiting the Mayan ruins at Palenque, one of Mexico's top attractions (*see pp104–5*). However, there are two museums that should on no account be missed.

CICOM

This is the acronym for the **Centro de Investigaciones de las Culturas Olmeca y Maya**, an anthropological research centre specialising in the Olmec and Maya civilisations. Within

THE OLMECS

The 'people from the land of rubber' (in Náhuatl) are seen as the forerunners of all pre-Columbian civilisations. They developed a culture around the Gulf Coast which flourished between about 1200 and 400 BC. These were the first known people to build pyramid bases for temples, which remained as basic mounds of earth. They also developed a numerical system and glyphic script.

The Olmecs worked with jade and precious stones, carved stone altars, sculptures and stelae, and are known for the great monolithic basalt heads found mainly in La Venta, San Lorenzo and Tres Zapotes. Thought to represent prominent leaders, the heads are carved with broad noses and thick lips. The Negroid-type characteristics continue to puzzle researchers investigating the origins of the Olmecs. The heads are on display in various museums.

this huge cultural complex is the **Carlos Pellicer Cámara Regional Anthropology Museum**, which houses a magnificent pre-Hispanic collection. *Calle Ocampo (on riverbank). Tel: (993) 312 6344. Open: Tue–Sun 9am–5pm. Admission charge (Sun & holidays free).*

Parque Museo de La Venta

Back in the 1950s, Olmec sculptures were brought to this unique open-air park museum from the archaeological site of La Venta, 95km (59 miles) away, where oilfields were being developed. Some 30 items are displayed in a jungle setting very like they would have been originally. The main attraction is three colossal basalt-stone heads with heavy, Negroid-type features and 'helmets'. (There are more monolith heads in the Museums of Anthropology in Jalapa, Veracruz and Mexico City.) The facial characteristics of these sculptures have provoked continuing speculation about the origins of the Olmec people. There is a small zoo in the park, as well as many free-roaming animals, and you may well come across monkeys, deer, the odd tapir and perhaps coatimundis (relatives of the racoon), which appear at the first sign of any food. Remember to use insect repellent.

Blvd Ruiz Cortines, near Paseo Tabasco. Tel: (993) 314 1652. Open: daily 8am–5pm. Admission charge.

Villahermosa is 860km (534 miles) southeast of Mexico City. Information office: Paseo Tabasco 1504. Tel: (993) 316 3633. Flights from Mexico City and other domestic destinations. Well connected by bus.

NEARBY

The most westerly of the ancient Mayan cities was **Comalcalco**, 60km (37 miles) northwest of Villahermosa, which flourished between AD 800 and 1250. The site was not of stone, but of sun-baked bricks and mortar made of sand, clay and ground oyster shells.
Open: daily 10am–4pm. Admission charge (Sun & holidays are free).

Villahermosa

Olmec head, La Venta: a party of schoolchildren see a piece of their history

Northern Mexico

The area loosely called northern Mexico stretches from the Gulf of California in the west to the Gulf of Mexico in the east. The Río Bravo (or Río Grande) forms the greater part of the country's border with the US.

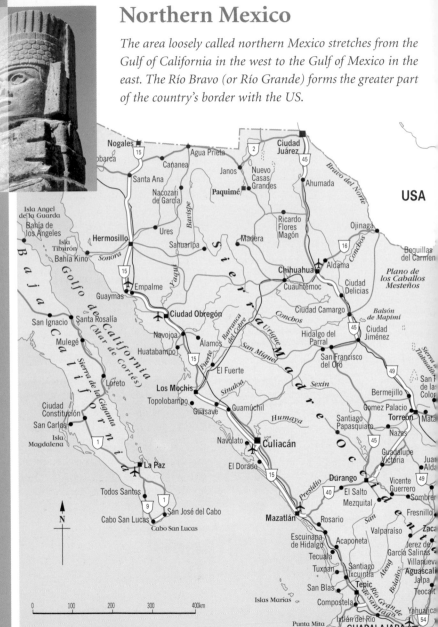

USA

Nogales
barca
Agua Prieta
Ciudad Juárez
Bravo del Norte
Cananea
Janos
Nuevo Casas Grandes
Paquimé
Ahumada
Santa Ana
Nacozari de García
Ricardo Flores Magón
Ojinaga
Isla Angel de la Guarda
Bahía de los Ángeles
Hermosillo
Ures
Madera
Boquillas del Carmen
Isla Tiburón
Bahía Kino
Sonora
Sahuaripa
Chihuahua
Aldama
Plano de los Caballos Mesteños
Sierra Madre
Cuauhtémoc
Ciudad Delicias
Empalme
Guaymas
Conchos
Ciudad Camargo
Balsón de Mapimí
Ciudad Obregón
Barranca del Cobre
Urique
Hidalgo del Parral
Ciudad Jiménez
Navojoa
Álamos
San Miguel
San Ignacio
Santa Rosalía
Huatabampo
Fuerte
El Fuerte
San Francisco del Oró
Sierra de Tlahualila
de la Color
Mulegé
Sinaloa
Sexin
Bermejillo
Loreto
Los Mochis
Topolobampo
Guasave
Guamúchil
Humaya
Gomez Palacio
Torreón
Mata
Ciudad Constitución
San Carlos
Navolato
Culiacán
Santiago Papasquiaro
Nazas
Isla Magdalena
El Dorado
Guadalupe Victoria
Juan Alda
La Paz
Dúrango
Vicente Guerrero
Todos Santos
El Salto
Mezquital
Sombrer
San José del Cabo
Mazatlán
Rosario
Fresnillo
Cabo San Lucas
Escuinapa de Hidalgo
Acaponeta
Valparaíso
Zaca
Tecuala
Jerez de García Salinas
Villanueva
Aguascali
Jalpa
Tuxpan
Santiago Ixcuintla
San Blas
Tepic
Teocalt
Islas Marías
Compostela
Río Grande de Santiago
Yahualica
Punta Mita
Ixtlán del Río
GUADALAJARA

0 100 200 300 400km

This is a region of arid lands, lofty mountains and plateaus. The Sierra Madre Oriental and Sierra Madre Occidental run parallel to the eastern and western coasts respectively. Between the ranges is a high plain where Mexico's major cities lie. The state of Sonora, in the northwestern corner, is characterised by deserts, populated largely by cacti. Experience the incomparable beauty of the desert meeting the sea at the rapidly developing resort of Puerto Peñasco at the northern end of the Sea of Cortés.

Further south is the quiet village of Bahía Kino. The Seris, one of the few surviving pure Indian tribes in Mexico, live here, surviving by selling polished ironwood pieces and huge, handwoven baskets. San Carlos is 400km (249 miles) south, in Baja California, surrounded by jagged desert peaks. It boasts of one of the most perfect natural harbours.

The north is renowned for its cattle raising, and huge ranches are located in Sonora, in Chihuahua and around San Luis Potosí, further south. It is also a rich mining area, and serves as the base for an increasing number of assembly plants for US products.

Monterrey is an important industrial centre, and also a major producer of beer. Although it is not tourist country, many of its attractions are unique. Giant saguaro and other cacti stand sentinel across the great Sonoran deserts. The countryside around Monterrey and Durango is lonely and wild, suited to the many 'Westerns' filmed there. A rail journey through the breathtaking Barranca del Cobre (Copper Canyon), in Chihuahua, offers side-trips deep down into the canyons, and a glimpse of the Tarahumara Indians (*see pp140–41*).

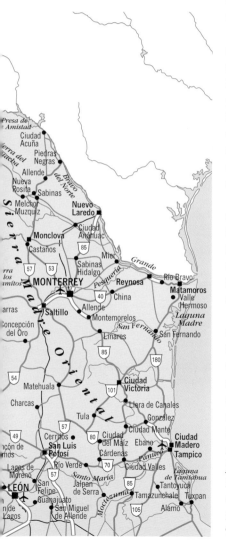

Chihuahua

Capital of the largest and one of the richest states in Mexico, Chihuahua is a major agricultural, cattle and industrial centre, with the maquiladora *industry now also big business. The place exudes an air of affluence, with a noticeable influence from across the border. Modern buildings contrast with old traditional homes, and well-heeled ranchers are seen about town. Chihuahua is the starting or finishing point for the famous Copper Canyon railway trip (see pp140–41).*

Historically, the area has seen much turbulence. The Spaniards expended a lot of time and effort to settle it, as it was continuously under attack from Apache and Comanche Indians. These tribes hindered the town's development after silver mining began at the start of the 18th century. Independence hero Father Miguel Hidalgo and some of his band were captured and executed here in 1811. The town was occupied for short periods by US troops during the 1846–8 war with the United States, and the War of Intervention (1862–6). In 1913, during the Mexican Revolution, the legendary Pancho Villa established his headquarters here, capturing the town by disguising his men as peasants.
Chihuahua is 375km (233 miles) south of Ciudad Juárez on the US border. Information office: Palacio de Gobierno, Planta Baja. Tel: (614) 429 3300 & freephone (01 800) 849 5200. www.chihuahua.gob.mx. Flights from Mexico City, other domestic destinations and the US. Regular bus connections from Mexico City and US border towns. Trains to Ciudad Juárez, Mexico City and Los Mochis (through the Copper Canyon).

Catedral Metropolitana

Dominating the main square is the twin-towered cathedral. Completed in 1826, it has a magnificent Baroque façade and an elaborate interior of gold and marble.
Plaza de Armas. Open: daily 10am–8pm. Admission charge.

Museo de la Revolución 'Quinta Luz'

Also known simply as Casa Villa (Villa's House), this is the former home and headquarters of the famous, heroic Pancho Villa. Photographs, furniture, weapons and relics evoke the atmosphere of the revolution and recall the bold life of the bandit-turned-general. The most dramatic exhibit is the bullet-holed Dodge in which he and

his companions were assassinated in 1923. The museum was established after his death by his widow, Luz Corral, who looked after it until her death in 1981.
Calle Décima. Tel: (614) 416 2958. Open: Tue–Sat 9am–1pm & 3–7pm, Sun 9am–5pm. Admission charge.

Palacio de Gobierno

The Governor's Palace is where Father Hidalgo was executed by a firing squad during the Independence War. At the Fatherland's Altar, built on the very spot of his execution, flickers an eternal flame.
Opposite Plaza Hidalgo. Tel: (614) 429 3596. Open: daily 9am–7pm.

CHIHUAHUA ENVIRONS

Casas Grandes, also known as **Paquimé**, is the most important archaeological site in northern Mexico. Although evidence suggests a much earlier occupation, its culture is believed to have flourished between AD 900 and 1100. In the 14th century the place was destroyed by nomadic tribes. The site includes the adobe ruins of community houses, underground water channels, a large ball court and a central plaza.

Located west of Chihuahua is **Cuauhtémoc**, a cattle and farming town. The surrounding area is inhabited by a Mennonite colony. A visit provides a glimpse of the life of these people, who came here in the early 1920s (*see p140*).
Casas Grandes: 270km (168 miles) northwest of Chihuahua. Open: Tue–Sun 10am–5pm. Tel: (636) 692 4140. Admission charge.
Cuauhtémoc: 105km (65 miles) west of Chihuahua.

Chihuahua's splendid cathedral: its completion was delayed by continual Indian raids

DURANGO

Founded in 1563, Durango flourished when gold, silver and other minerals were found here in the 18th and 19th centuries. Designated a national historic monument, the state capital has attractive colonial architecture.

Casa de los Condes de Súchil

This 18th-century residence has a façade of carved stone; inside, an enormous Moorish arch leads to the main patio with its double arcade.
5 de Febrero 32.

Catedral

Begun in the late 17th century, this structure is primarily Baroque in style. Note the pretty ironwork on the left tower, and the finely carved images on the choir stalls.
North side of the main square.

Palacio de Gobierno

This 18th-century Governor's Palace originally belonged to a wealthy miner. Its colonial-style arcades are decorated with murals depicting Durango's history.
Zaragoza 5 de Febrero.

Villa del Oeste

A special attraction for film fans are the old sets from the time when Westerns were produced *en masse* here. About 14km (8½ miles) north of the city are two 'cowboy towns' – wooden houses and verandas, saloons and bars, and the open square – seen in many a John Wayne film. These can be visited on

The film sets of many Hollywood Westerns can be visited near Durango

tours at weekends (*contact your hotel or local tourist office to arrange a visit*). *598km (372 miles) north of Guadalajara. Information office: Florida 1006. Tel: (618) 811 1107. Buses from Mexico City, Guadalajara and Mazatlán. Though connected by rail, the services are slow.*

MONTERREY

Monterrey is Nuevo León's state capital and Mexico's third-largest city. It sprawls over a large valley dominated by the imposing Cerro de la Silla (Saddle Mountain), the symbol of the city. Although a modern industrial centre, it still retains vestiges of colonial charm, with narrow streets and cool, inviting courtyards. The Gran Plaza is an unusually spacious square containing government buildings, fountains, sculptures and theatres, all exhibiting a contrast of styles.

Cervecería Cuauhtémoc

Monterrey is famous for its production of beer. The Cuauhtémoc Brewery,

founded in the late 19th century, developed into a major enterprise.
Avenida Universidad 2202. Tel: (81) 8328 5355. Open: Mon–Fri 9am–5pm, Sat 9am–2pm. Tours by request.

Museo de Arte Contemporáneo

Known as MARCO, this well-designed building hosts outstanding temporary exhibits of contemporary art.
Gran Plaza. Tel: (81) 8342 4820. Open: Tue & Thur–Sun 10am–6pm, Wed 10am–8pm. Admission charge.

Museo de Historia Mexicana

This new museum gives an insight into the history of Mexico's 1910 revolution. A river walk, cafés and boat ride add to the attraction.
Dr Coss 445 Sur. Tel: (81) 8345 9898. Open: Wed–Fri 10am–7pm, Sat–Sun 10am–8pm. Admission charge.

ENVIRONS

Impressive natural attractions include the **Grutas de García** (García Caves) 45km (28 miles) west, with stalagmite and stalactite formations, a subterranean lake and 16 lighted caverns; the **Cola de Caballo** (Horsetail Falls), 40km (25 miles) south, where a wooded path beside a stream cuts through a ravine to the base of the falls; **Cañon de Huasteca** (Huasteca Canyon), 10km ($6^{1}/4$ miles) south, with sheer rock walls rising out of the landscape; and the **Chipinque Mesa**, 19km (12 miles) southwest, a popular picnic spot.

Monterrey is 963km (598 miles) north of Mexico City. Information office: Antiguo Palacio Federal. Tel: (81) 344 4343. www.turismomonterrey.com.
Flights from Mexico City, other Mexican destinations and the US. Bus and rail connections.

Neptune emerges from a Monterrey fountain

SAN LUIS POTOSI

Situated right in the heart of cattle-ranching country, this old mining town has a very Mexican flavour. Although not on the tourist track, it has considerable charm, and some fine buildings, mostly clustered near the heart of the city. After silver and gold were found in the area at the end of the 16th century, San Luis became one of the most important towns in Mexico. Evidence of the town's past wealth can be seen in its fine colonial buildings and attractive squares.

417km (259 miles) north of Mexico City. Information office: Alvaro Obregon 520. Tel: (444) 812 9939. Bus connections to Mexico City, Monterrey and León.

Catedral

The 17th-century twin-towered cathedral has an impressive Baroque façade, with a porch adorned by statues of the twelve Apostles. Its interior is composed of various styles.

Plaza de Armas.

Museo Regional Potosino

Housed in the former Franciscan convent, this regional museum houses some fine archaeological pieces, and a fine Churrigueresque chapel upstairs.

Galeana 450. Tel: (444) 814 3572. Open: Tue–Sat 10am–7pm, Sun 10am–5pm. Admission charge.

Templo del Carmen

Perhaps the most interesting of the city's churches, this Carmelite building is noted for its Baroque façade, grand tiled dome and richly adorned interior.

Plaza del Carmen.

Templo de San Francisco

The interior of this 17th-century church has scenes from the life of St Francis, as well as an unusual chandelier shaped like a ship, suspended over the apse, and said to have been donated by a shipwreck survivor. The sacristy is outstanding.

Plaza San Francisco. Open: daily 7am–2pm, 4–9pm.

ZACATECAS

Set at high altitude in hilly terrain at the foot of the Cerro de la Bufa, the state capital is surrounded by agricultural and ranching land. It dates from the 16th century, when Spaniards discovered rich deposits of silver, copper and zinc nearby. Great quantities of silver were shipped to Spain to finance their explorations around the world, and the town flourished for the next three centuries. Elegant colonial mansions and churches bear testimony to this affluence. Today, this picturesque city of pink-stone houses is still a silver mining centre, with a colonial heritage as yet unspoilt by tourism. Its narrow, cobblestone streets, alleyways and handsome buildings make it rewarding to explore on foot.

613km (381 miles) north of Mexico City. Information office: Avenida Hidalgo, 403, 2nd Fl. Tel: (492) 924 0552.

www.turismozacatecas.gob.mx. Flights from Mexico City, Tijuana and Los Angeles. Buses from Mexico City and Guadalajara. Freephone Infotur: (01 800) 712 4078.

Catedral

The cathedral stands out as one of Mexico's finest examples of the Churrigueresque style. Its rose-coloured façade is adorned with elaborate carvings, crowned by a figure of Christ flanked by the twelve Apostles. The interior, by contrast, is in plain Neo-Classical style.

Plaza de Armas.

Cerro de la Bufa

The summit of the hill that dominates Zacatecas can best be reached by the *teleférico*, the Swiss-made aerial cable-car that climbs to the chapel at the top. A renowned pilgrimage site, it has magnificent views of the entire city, and a museum on Pancho Villa.

Museum open: Tue–Sun 10am–4.30pm. Admission charge.

Mina del Edén

Mini-trains tour the abandoned 16th-century Eden Mine. The adventurous can cross a hanging bridge over one of the shafts. By night the place becomes a disco.

Northeast of town, near the hospital. Tel: (492) 922 3002. Open: daily 10am–6pm. Admission charge.

Museo Pedro Coronel

Housed in a former Jesuit monastery, the museum contains a fine collection of artworks donated by the Zacatecan artist Pedro Coronel.

Plaza Santo Domingo. Tel: (492) 922 8021. Open: Fri–Wed 10am–4.30pm. Admission charge.

Palacio del Gobierno

This handsome 18th-century building, now the Town Hall, once served as a residence for some of the Zacatecan nobility. Worth seeing are the attractive courtyard and historical mural.

East side of Plaza de Armas.

Templo de Santo Domingo

St Dominic's Church, the richest in Zacatecas, dates back to the mid-18th century. It was built on massive foundations on difficult, uneven terrain.

Calle Codina.

Church detail in Cerro de la Bufa

Baja California

Some 20 million years ago, seismic upheavals along the San Andreas Fault caused a narrow finger of land to separate from the mainland of Mexico. The waters of the Pacific filled the gap – now called the Gulf of California or the Mar de Cortés – and formed the long peninsula known as Baja (Lower) California.

From the US border in the north to its southernmost point, Baja California peninsula is some 1,300km (808 miles) long. It averages about 90km (56 miles) across and at its widest is only 193km (120 miles).

The giant cacti of Baja California

The area was originally inhabited by various Indian groups. A number of prehistoric cave paintings have been found here, the most significant of which are those around San Ignacio. Hernán Cortés first came here in 1535 to what became La Paz, but it took time and effort to settle the region. Jesuit priests were sent here in the 17th century, and gradually succeeded in converting the native Indians to Christianity. During the 19th century foreigners bought land and established large ranches. Fishing, which is big business today, began in earnest.

Often simply called Baja, the peninsula is divided at the 28th parallel into two states, Baja California Norte (North), and Baja California Sur (South). Two high ranges run down its length: the Sierra San Pedro Martír, with pine and oak forests in the northern half, and the Sierra de la Giganta in the south. The central region is dominated by the **Desierto Vizcaíno** (Vizcaíno Desert), with landscapes of giant cacti, cirio trees and wind-polished boulders.

The area to the north is more agricultural, with valleys devoted to vineyards, olive groves, cotton and wheat, while the south is characterised by lush vegetation, fine sandy beaches and rugged rock formations against a warm, emerald sea. Tourism is growing, but Baja still offers untouched expanses of natural beauty and a climate that is reliably dry and pleasant all year round. *www.turismobc.gob.mx*

Baja California

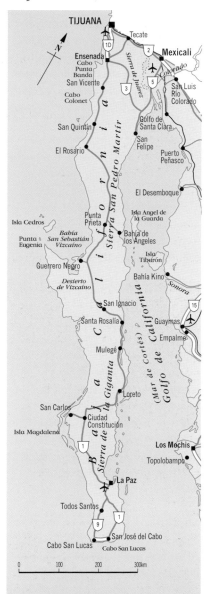

Baja California

Baja California

BAJA CALIFORNIA NORTE
Ensenada

This delightful, busy seaport is the nearest major beach resort to Tijuana, and a long-time favourite with both Mexicans and southern Californians. It offers fine sandy beaches, good deep-sea fishing, sailing, surfing and a casino. The surrounding area is wine country, and visits to the wineries of Cavas Valmar or Bodegas de Santo Tomás, the oldest on the peninsula, can be arranged (ask at your hotel or the tourist office). Crafts from all over Mexico – silver, pottery and *serapes* (colourful woven blankets) – are reasonably priced.

Some 35km (22 miles) southwest of Ensenada is **Cabo Punta Banda**, where the mountains meet the sea. Here, over the centuries, the pounding surf has formed a hole through which the waves crash with tremendous power, forcing the water up to a great height. The loud noise it makes gave it its name, **La Bufadora** (The Snorting One).
108km (67 miles) south of Tijuana. Information office: Blvd Costera 1477. Tel: (646) 178 2411. www.enjoyensenada.com. Car or bus from Tijuana, Mexicali and other centres.

Mexicali

Mexicali, capital of Baja California Norte, is a busy border town oriented more towards business than tourism. However, there are a couple of places worth a visit, especially the museum.
On the US border, 169km (105 miles)

The spectacular blowhole – La Bufadora – at Cabo Punta de la Banda

east of Tijuana. Information office: Calz Montejano 1. Tel: (686) 566 1277. Flights from Mexico City, other Mexican destinations and the US. Bus connections to Mexico City and other Mexican destinations. Rail services to Mexico City and Guadalajara.

Museo Regional de la Universidad Autónoma

Exhibits display Baja's archaeology, culture, history and missions.
Avenida Reforma. Tel: (686) 554 1977. Open: Mon–Fri 9am–6pm, Sat–Sun 10am–4pm. Admission charge.

San Felipe

From a picturesque fishing and shrimping port, San Felipe has grown into a favourite beach resort for US visitors. It lies on the Gulf of California, against majestic rocky mountains and inland desert. Its long sandy beaches bustle with cars and campers at weekends, and during the tourist season. Condominiums and hotels line the waterfront. San Felipe is also popular for sport fishing.

200km (124 miles) south of Mexicali. Information office: Mar de Cortés and Manzanillo. Buses to Mexicali and Ensenada.

Tijuana

Formerly a notorious border town, Tijuana has largely cleaned up its act and no longer merits its 'Sin City' image. A better nickname might be 'Fun City'. A 30-minute drive or so from San Diego leads to another world – of colour, noise, chaos and fun.

According to statistics, Tijuana receives more US visitors annually than any other foreign city in the world. Many visitors cross the border just to enjoy the restaurants, bars and nightclubs. Discount prices in this duty-free zone attract hordes of day shoppers.

Tijuana also offers many sporting attractions such as *jai alai* (*see p160*), bullfights, horse and dog racing, rodeos and baseball.

Tijuana Centro Cultural

This attractively designed, modern complex contains a history museum, temporary exhibits and local handicrafts, in addition to the spectacular Omnimax movie cinema.

Paseo de los Héroes and Avenida Independencia. Tel: (664) 687 9600. Open: daily 9am–8pm. Admission charge.

Tijuana is on the US border, 25km (15½ miles) south of San Diego. Information office: Paseo Los Heroes y Jose Ma Velasco. Tel: (664) 684 0537. www.seetijuana.com. Also at Edif Nafinsa, 4th Fl, Avenida Revolución y Calle Primera. Flights from Mexico City, LA and other Mexican and US destinations. Bus service from Mexico City and other Mexican destinations.

Baja California

The Bodegas de Santo Tomás offer cellar tours and wine tastings

Whale watching

Every autumn thousands of California grey whales migrate south from the Bering Strait off the Alaskan coast to central Baja's Pacific coast. Hunted nearly to extinction by 1946 and now dramatically recovered in numbers, these stately giants – as long as 15m (49ft) and weighing between 20 and 40 tonnes when mature – take two to three months to make the 9,500km (5,900-mile) journey. In the warm, tranquil lagoons, they court, mate, snort and cavort in an amorous free-for-all, while females give birth to calves conceived the previous year in shallower waters.

Each baby is born weighing 750–1,000kg (¾–1 ton) and measures about 5m long (16½ft); suckling its mother's rich milk (53 per cent fat), the calf doubles its weight and adds another metre (3¼ft) to its length by the end of the winter. Adults begin heading back north in March, with the calves – strenuously 'trained' at the mouth of the lagoon – following on with their mothers as late as May or June.

Taking a peek at the grey whales' intimate domestic life is an intriguing and ever more popular pastime. The main whale sanctuaries where these giant mammals display their antics are Scammon's Lagoon (named after the Maine whaler who found the breeding ground in 1857), Laguna San Ignacio and Magdalena Bay. The first is about 40km (25 miles) from Guerrero Negro, a town just below the border that

divides Baja into north and south, and services one of the world's largest salt evaporation works. Magdalena Bay is the best place to see whales, since it is the most accessible from La Paz, and is geared to whale watching.

In 1960, Scammon's Lagoon, also known as Ojo de Liebre (Eye of the Hare), was declared a Grey Whale Natural Park; this and its sister lagoon at Guerrero Negro were the first such sanctuaries in the world. Laguna San Ignacio, 200km (124 miles) further south, gained similar status in 1979 (*see p143*).

For the closest possible encounter, boat trips on the lagoons can be arranged locally; for the more timid, a pair of binoculars on the shore should do nicely.

Magdalena Bay is a good place to spot whales in the winter months

Loreto's mission church sent forth the friars who founded the chain of California missions

BAJA CALIFORNIA SUR
La Paz

La Paz (Peace) has a pleasant *malecón* (seafront promenade) and beach and a busy port; its free port status means there are plenty of bargains to be had. Large passenger and car ferries depart for Mazatlán and Topolobampo on the mainland from Pichilingue, 16km (10 miles) north.

The waters of La Paz once supported a thriving pearl-fishing business (John Steinbeck's story *The Pearl* is said to have been based on a tale he heard here in 1941). However, in 1940, a mysterious epidemic wiped out the oysters, and all but killed off the town as well. Later, regular ferry services to the mainland improved airport facilities, and a paved Transpeninsular Highway gave it the necessary impetus for its revival.

In spite of much growth, there are enough arched doorways and flower-filled patios that retain the graceful character of old La Paz. Many businesses, especially in summer, observe the traditional afternoon siesta. By night, the *zócalo*, brilliantly illuminated with old pebble-glass globes, is a rare sight.

The **Anthropological Museum** has good displays of the region's geology, history, prehistory and folklore. A series of beautiful beaches stretching up the coast offers good snorkelling and fishing and some stunning sunsets. *1,384km (860 miles) south of Tijuana. Information office: Paseo Obregon. Tel: (612) 124 0103.*
Anthropological Museum: Cinco de Mayo and Altamirano. Tel: (612) 122 0162. Open: Mon–Fri 9am–6pm, Sat 9am–1pm. Free admission. Flights from Mexico City, other Mexican destinations and the US.

Loreto

The first permanent settlement in Baja California was founded here by the Jesuits in 1697. Loreto became the peninsula's first capital, but lost this status in 1830 after the town was devastated by a hurricane. Time seems to have stood still in this historic place. The town has a few shady squares and a pleasant *malecón*. The project for a tourist development south of Loreto has produced a new golf course, with plans for additional accommodation. *356km (221 miles) north of La Paz. Air connections from Mexico City, Tijuana and Los Angeles. Buses from Tijuana and La Paz.*

Misión de Nuestra Señora de Loreto

This well-restored, early 18th-century mission church on the *zócalo* has a small adjoining museum, the Museo de los Misiones, which depicts local history, culture and mission activities. *Zócalo open: Tue–Fri 9am–1pm and 1.45–6pm.*

Los Cabos

Los Cabos (The Capes) is the name given to the southernmost part of the peninsula, divided into the two resorts of San José del Cabo and Cabo San Lucas. The area has seen considerable development over recent years, and a variety of attractive hotels is strung along the stretch of coastline known as the 'corridor', which is characterised by long sandy beaches, dramatic rock formations and coves. The setting of desert, mountains and sea, combined

The busy harbour of Cabo San Lucas

with good fishing, aquatic sports and top-class golf courses, gives the area a special appeal.

Cabo San Lucas

Once a sheltering place for treasure ships from the Orient, as well as for pirates, this is a lively resort with an increasing supply of hotels, restaurants and nightspots. The harbour, with its large fishing fleet and open-air market, is always busy. It is internationally renowned for year-round sport-fishing; charter arrangements can be made on the waterfront or through many of the hotels. Distinctive black coral jewellery is made and sold at the regional arts centre at the cruise liner dock. Sandy beaches, blue-green seas and a coastline of volcanic formations offer good swimming, surfing, scuba diving and snorkelling, as well as waterskiing, parasailing, windsurfing and volleyball. Golf and tennis are also available.

Visitors should take a boat trip to the striking rock formation known as **El Arco** (The Arch). The area is rich in marine life and favoured by divers. At

French architectural influences

the point where the Pacific meets the Gulf lies the secluded **Playa de Amor** (Love Beach), popular for swimming and picnics.

San José del Cabo

This small trading and tourist centre has a shady main square, shops, a few hotels and a mission-style church – a place to visit rather than to stay in. The real holiday area is the hotel zone that has developed within the community. Hotels, condominiums and villas stretch along the coast.

Los Cabos is located at the south of the peninsula, 216km (134 miles) south of La Paz. Flights from Mexico City, other Mexican destinations and the US. Bus connections to La Paz. Cabo San Lucas is also a port of call for ocean liners.

Mulegé

This delightful little tropical oasis, with its hilltop mission church, lies on an estuary a few kilometres from the Gulf. With its narrow streets, thatched roofs and date palms first planted by the Jesuits, it has great charm and is a popular stopover for travellers exploring the peninsula. South of town, a short distance away, are some attractive beaches along Bahía Concepción. There are charter fishing trips to nearby islands, and good diving and snorkelling. Guided excursions are available to see ancient cave paintings near San Baltazar and San Patricio; San Borjita Cave contains an interesting collection of petroglyphs, but is less accessible. It is best to go with a local guide.

495km (308 miles) north of La Paz. Buses from Tijuana to La Paz stop here.

Santa Rosalía

Ever since its founding in 1855 by a French-owned copper-mining company, Santa Rosalía has retained a certain Gallic flavour, its picturesque wooden houses and long verandas distinctly influenced by the French colonial style. The focal point of the town is the harbour, which serves as a terminal for regular car ferries across to Guaymas on the mainland.

During World War I, Germany's Pacific sailing fleet was interned here for the entire duration of the war. The Palacio Municipal is a fine example of French architecture. The most impressive landmark in the town, however, is the 19th-century church, thought to have been designed by Gustave Eiffel (of Eiffel Tower fame), constructed of prefabricated galvanised iron in France and shipped over here. Railway enthusiasts will like the relics of the metre-gauge steam-powered railway that served the mines and smelter until the late 19th century. One locomotive can be seen in the town centre, and more equipment is displayed outdoors about 500m (550yds) north along the highway. Nearby beaches of Santa María and San Lucas offer good swimming.

65km (40 miles) north of Mulegé. Buses from Tijuana and La Paz.

Getting away from it all

A country the size of Mexico is bound to offer many exciting and diverse opportunities for those who seek something out of the ordinary. Lakeside resorts, spas and beautiful national parks beckon those who seek peace and tranquillity. For the more adventurous there is much to explore. Ecotourism, nature-related travel with a low impact on the environment, is becoming increasingly popular.

Caves and *cenotes*

Dotted about the countryside are a number of caves (*grutas*) with stunning stalactite and stalagmite formations. Never explore on your own. Always take a guide or join a tour, and definitely heed warning signs.

Northeast of Taxco are the **Grutas de Cacahuamilpa** (Cacahuamilpa Caves), noted for their spectacular rock formations. In the vicinity you can visit the **Grutas de Estrella** (Star Grottoes) and the **Grutas de Juxtlahuaca** (Juxtlahuaca Caves), southeast of Chilpancingo. The **Coconá Caves**, 56km (35 miles) south of Villahermosa, are also known for their striking limestone formations.

Among Yucatán's most impressive caves are the **Grutas de Loltún** (Loltún Grottoes), south of Mérida, which contain Mayan wall paintings and stone artefacts; those of Calcehtok, further west, with lofty vaults and underground streams; and the **Balancanché Cave**, 5km (3 miles) east

of Chichén Itzá, with a small lake and more Mayan relics.

Some of the *cenotes* (sinkholes) offer excellent snorkelling or merely a refreshing swim in an unusual setting. Among the most attractive are those at Dzitnup near Valladolid, Chen-Ha, southwest of Mérida, and Xtogil, some 20km (12½ miles) east of Chichén Itzá. At Xcaret (*see p96*), south of Cancún, an underground river passes through impressive submerged caverns that served as sacred *cenotes*. By the **Cenote Azul** on the shores of Laguna Bacalar, north of Chetumal, you can swim or enjoy excellent seafood at the *palapa*-roofed restaurant while watching young boys dive into waters of stunning clarity. The most famous of them all is the **Cenote de los Sacrificios** in Chichén Itzá (*see pp98–9*), where virgins are said to have been sacrificed to the rain god. This one, however, is not for swimming!

Ask your hotel or contact the local tourist office for more information.

Visits to some of the caves, grottoes and *cenotes* are included in organised excursions.

Deserts and jungles

The desertlands of northern Mexico and Baja California can provide the perfect, unexpected refuge. The great **Sonoran Desert** in the northwest, extending well into the US, offers 'Arizona-type' vistas with giant cacti silhouetted against a brilliant blue sky. Baja California offers an appealing contrast of desert, sea and mountains, with some wild terrain in the peninsula's interior challenging your determination to arrive. The **Cataviña Natural Park**, south of El Rosario, offers some of the most bizarre scenery in Baja: giant boulders among hectares of weirdly shaped cirio trees and great cardon cacti.

An on-foot experience of a tropical jungle is the stuff of many people's fantasies. In the jungle regions of southeastern Mexico, you can easily combine such a trek with a visit to Mayan ruins or other centres. Archaeological sites like Palenque (*see pp104–5*), Bonampak and Yaxchilán (*see p103*) are buried deep in the jungle. Kohunlich, near Chetumal, is surrounded by massive kapok trees and magnificent palms; Becán, Chicanná and Balankú, among many other archaeological sites in Campeche, offer walks into the engulfing vegetation. For the less adventurous, the open-air **museum of La Venta** in Villahermosa

(*see p113*) and the excellent **Zoomat** in Tuxtla Gutiérrez (*see p159*) are both in exotic jungle surroundings.

Interesting jungle excursions and riding expeditions are organised from Puerto Vallarta (*see pp88–9*) and Mazatlán (*see p86*), across the bay. Do not venture into the jungle without a guide; stick to marked trails – and take plenty of good insect repellent and bottled water.

Sturdy, pillar-like Joshua palms pose jauntily against the desert sky of Nuevo León

In Yucatán, mysteriously evocative waters ripple in a sacred *cenote* at Ozibilichaltun

Hiking and climbing

If you are looking for relaxed walking in the countryside, visit any of the national parks, where marked paths lead through beautiful surroundings. From Mexico City you can make day trips to the national parks of Desierto de los Leones, Ajusco, Lagunas de Zempoala, Izta-Popo and Nevado de Toluca, all of which offer cool pine forests, lakes and fresh mountain air.

For dedicated hikers who wish to get off the beaten track, there are countless possibilities depending on your interests. The Barranca del Cobre (Copper Canyon) region in northwestern Mexico offers awesome landscapes and splendid isolation. (Treks down into the canyons should not be attempted without the services of a local guide.) In the highlands of Chiapas, following the trails from one village to another gives a fascinating glimpse of local life. As a contrast, the flat scrub-lands of the Yucatán make for pleasant walking, and can be combined with visits to lesser-known Mayan ruins and wildlife refuges. For those with time to spare, it is even possible to walk right around the peninsula of Baja California – it has been done!

Mountaineering, in the true sense of the word, is limited in Mexico. Very little rock climbing is possible, owing to the unsuitable texture of the rocks at high altitudes. The three tallest peaks in Mexico – Orizaba, Popocatépetl and Iztaccíhuatl – are often climbed (although, after it erupted, climbing Popocatépetl was halted). However, all require a great deal of fitness and stamina, if not first-class mountaineering skills. La Malinche and Nevado de Colima volcanoes are also popular mountain climbs.

RIVERS AND RAFTING

A boat trip on the Grijalva River through the Cañon del Sumidero (Sumidero Canyon) passes between walls of sheer rock (*see p103*). Boarding points are Cuaharé or Chiapa de Corzo (east of Tuxtla Gutiérrez).

River trips into the jungle hinterland can also be taken from Villahermosa, Tenocique (Tabasco) and Champotón (Campeche). Ecogrupos de México (Eugenia 13-702, Col. Napoles, Mexico City, *tel: (55) 5687 6255*) offers tours including boat trips through the Sumidero Canyon and on the Usumacinta River.

White-water rafting: on Veracruz's rivers (best June–Oct); San Luis Potosí (Nov–Mar only). Contact Expediciones México Verde. *Tel: (279) 832 3730* in México City, *freephone (01 800) 3628 800. www.mexicoverde.com.* You can also raft down the rapids of Papagayo River (*see p79*).

For more information contact: CAM (Club Alpino Méxicano), Coahuila 40, Col. Roma. Tel: (55) 5574 9683. www.clubalpinomexicano.com.mx

Lakes, lagoons and rivers

The shores of some of Mexico's lakes, each with its own distinctive personality, are havens of peace and quiet. The largest is Lake Chapala. The town of Chapala (*see p52*) has a lively promenade of bars, restaurants and *mariachi* bands. For a calmer existence, try the quaint little lakeside villages of Ajijic or Jocotepec, which attract the artistic set.

Lake Pátzcuaro (*see p63*), southwest of Morelia in neighbouring Michoacán, has a much quieter appeal. You can take a launch across to the curious cone-shaped island of Janitzio, or explore some of the tiny Tarascan communities around the lakeside.

South of Mexico City is a lovely region of lakes and forests contained within Parque Nacional Lagunas de Zempoala (Zempoala National Park). A little further, near Cuernavaca, is Lake Tequesquitengo, which offers boating and aquatic sports (weekdays are normally quiet). For something unusual, try the crater lake of Catemaco, 10km (6¼ miles) southeast of San Andrés Tuxtla in Veracruz; boat trips can be made to an islet inhabited by monkeys. The area is known for its witchcraft, and people come here to have a spell cast or a curse removed!

In the Yucatán there are some enchanting lagoons, such as Xel-Há south of Cancún (*see p96*) or the Chancanab lagoon on Cozumel island (*see p96*). Most spectacular are the Lagunas de Montebello (*see p103*), in Chiapas near Guatemala, a complex of some 60 lagoons, all in different hues.

Getting away from it all

A lazy day at the lakeside of Catemaco, formed in the crater of an old volcano

National parks

Mexico has over 50 national parks, covering mountainous, desert and jungle terrain. Some in the more central regions have marked paths, picnic areas, camping sites and lodges.

Several parks lie within the state of Mexico and are easily accessible from the capital. At **Lagunas de Zempoala**, seven turquoise lakes nestle in forested mountains. The romantic **Desierto de los Leones**, with its old Carmelite monastery, is set in thick pine and oak woods, while the extensive **Ajusco National Park** rests on the slopes of a dormant volcano. In Michoacán, the enchanting **Eduardo Ruiz National Park** sings with cascading streams and bubbling springs amid lush foliage. The Cupatitzio River rises here, and becomes a powerful 60m (197ft) high waterfall.

In the tropical regions of the southeast, parks often encompass a landmark of special note. At **Cascadas Agua Azul**, south of Palenque (*see p103*), you can swim amid sparkling cascades to the sound of tropical birds, while the multihued gorge of the **Cañon del Sumidero** (*see p103*) is the highlight of **Tuxtla Gutiérrez National Park**. Bordering Guatemala, the lakes of **Lagunas de Montebello National Park** (*see p103*) are set like dozens of vari-coloured gems in the orchid-laden wilderness.

In the parched lands of the north, **Cumbres de Monterrey National Park** features the sheer walls and bizarre rock formations of Huasteca Canyon.

A splashing fountain delights the eye and ear in Eduardo Ruiz National Park, Michoacán

Northwest of that lies the extraordinary **Copper Canyon National Park** (Barranca del Cobre, *see pp140–41*), with a series of deep, interconnecting gorges, which are considerably larger and deeper than Grand Canyon in the United States. At nearby **Basaseáchic Falls National Park**, the longest single-drop waterfall in North America tumbles through a natural ridge over a series of gigantic cliffs.

Mountain-spined Baja California has the **Sierra San Pedro Mártir National Park**, set in a vast plateau up in the peninsula's highest range of peaks. Trails and paths traverse meadows, streams and fragrant forests of pine, fir and juniper. Remote and relatively inaccessible, the park has a distinct appeal to the enterprising traveller. Enquire at your hotel or the local tourist office for information on how to reach these areas. Some of the parks are not easily accessible, and can only be reached by car.

Volcanoes

The snow-capped volcanoes that rise in the southern extreme of the central highlands are among Mexico's most outstanding features. Most famous are the pair known as Popocatépetl (Smoking Mountain) and Iztaccíhuatl (White Lady).

The higher Popocatépetl, according to legend, represents an Aztec warrior holding an eternal torch over his beloved Iztaccíhuatl, the princess who died of grief before he could return victorious from battle to claim her hand. On his return, he built two mountains, laid her body on one, and stood holding her funeral torch on the other. Different sections of Iztaccíhuatl are named after parts of her body. Further east lies the gentler-sloped **La Malinche volcano**, named after the famous Indian woman who was crucial in Cortés' conquest of Mexico, while in the coastal state of Veracruz rises **Pico de Orizaba**, Mexico's highest volcano at 5,700m (18,700ft). On the route from Mexico City through Puebla and Orizaba down to Veracruz, there are places where you can see all four peaks.

To the west lie the Nevado de Toluca, with two crater lakes, and the twins, **Volcán Nevado de Colima** and **Volcán de Fuego de Colima** (Mexico's most active volcano). A recent addition in Michoacán is the **Paricutín volcano**, which erupted without warning into a cornfield in 1943, and rose rapidly, engulfing two nearby villages in lava.

A solitary cross stands before the lake in the crater of the Nevado de Toluca volcano

Flora and fauna

With its geographical variety and different climatic zones, Mexico is blessed with a wealth of plant and animal life, both native and introduced over the centuries. Thousands of varieties of flowers, shrubs and trees surround you, adorning streets, courtyards and gardens. Travelling further afield, you will also come across a fantastic diversity of wildlife.

Tropical blossom and trees

In Mexico, you cannot escape the vibrant colours of nature. Widely seen are the many hues of bougainvillea, hibiscus, gold cup, frangipani and the red poinsettia or Christmas flower. Orchids are in a class of their own, and countless varieties grow in the regions around Veracruz. Bushes of pink oleander, mauve blossoms of the

A yellow-necked parrot

jacaranda tree and the magnificent blooms of the tulipan (African tulip tree) are integral to the Mexican scenery. Most striking are the vivid scarlet blossoms of the tabuchín tree, also known as the Flame Tree, whose bursts of colour brighten up even the most unexpected places.

Cacti in all their prickly forms – tall or squat, simple or multi-branched, rounded or gauntly angled – are a familiar sight. Dramatic cactus-strewn landscapes can be seen in the northwestern Sonoran Desert and in Baja California, which alone boasts 120 species. Cardons, the tallest, belong to the saguaro family from Arizona. Some cacti are put to practical use: the maguey for making *tequila* and *mezcal*, the *gobernadoras* for producing rubber, the *biznaga* (barrel cactus) for water in an emergency, and the *pitahaya dulce* (organ pipes) for nectar, once favoured by local Indians.

Vast tracts of forest characterise many parts of the country (although the clearing of the rainforest for cultivation in regions like Chiapas is the subject of some concern).
A great variety of trees, including the *ceiba* (kapok), palm trees, pine woods, bulrushes and mangroves

Prickly pear

abound, while plantations of sugar cane, coffee, cocoa beans and succulent tropical fruits crowd tropical coastal regions.

Wildlife

It is claimed that a thousand or so different species of birds have been recorded in Mexico. Birds of prey include species of hawks, vultures, kestrels and falcons. There are many graceful water birds, and in the Yucatán pink flamingos live in protected colonies. In a more domestic setting, you can observe woodpeckers and hovering hummingbirds in hotel gardens.

The southeastern jungles shelter members of the parrot family, including toucans and the brilliantly coloured *guacamayas* (macaws). A jewel among birds is the shy quetzal, which played an important role in Mayan mythology. Butterflies abound and can be seen in thousands at the butterfly sanctuaries in Michoacán (*see p143*).

The tropical forests of Chiapas are home to a host of animals including the jaguar, ocelot, lynx, tapir, howler and spider monkeys, coati and armadillos. Some of these are endangered species, and can be seen in the magnificent free-roaming zoo in Tuxtla Gutiérrez (*see p159*), which was created to protect the animals of the region. One remaining branch of the bear family, the small black bear, can still be found in several states of northern Mexico, as can wolves, elks and coyotes.

Baja California is the habitat of the elegant but rarely sighted mountain lion, or puma, and bighorn sheep live in remote desert areas. By the shores of that rugged peninsula you can also see colonies of California sea lions, and the large grey whales that come down every winter to breed in the lagoons on the Pacific. Aquatic animals are plentiful elsewhere, as well. The alligator (*caimán*) inhabits tropical rivers, and turtles are much in evidence in the Caribbean.

There are many species of snakes, among which are the deadly small coral snake (*coralillo*), rattlesnake (*cascabel*) and boa constrictor.

Huge areas of undeveloped land are being designated Biosphere Reserves by the Mexican government (*see pp142–3*), providing ideal conditions for observing wildlife in its natural habitat.

The Copper Canyon Railway journey

Those with a keen sense of adventure will enjoy a ride through the Barranca del Cobre, or Copper Canyon, in northwestern Mexico. As the Chihuahua Pacífico train travels between Los Mochis and Chihuahua through magnificent scenery, stopovers let you explore the rugged gorges inhabited by the Tarahumara Indians, who still live in caves, and many other areas of interest.

The line was completed in 1961, its railbed having been blasted from the side of the mountain for hundreds of kilometres. It has 39 bridges and 86 tunnels. A first-class train runs once daily in each direction between Los Mochis and Chihuahua, meeting midway at Divisadero. It's best to start from Los Mochis, to be sure of passing through the most scenic part of the journey in daylight.

The train makes a number of stops; locals get on and off, and vendors board to sell refreshments and handicrafts. The total journey time is about 14 hours – if there are no delays – but do allow time to explore the special attractions at stopovers like Divisadero, Creel and Cuauhtémoc.

The section between Los Mochis and Divisadero offers great vistas of jagged peaks, deep gorges and pine forests as the train makes its gradual ascent to the Copper Canyon. At Divisadero, a short walk takes you to the rim of the canyon, where the view into the mouths of three major canyons is a highlight of the journey. With an overnight stop, you can visit some of the Tarahumara caves and other nearby beauty spots.

Further along the line is the old lumber town of Creel. It makes a good base for excursions into the depths of the canyons, to the old mining areas of La Bufa and Batopilas. This is Tarahumara country, and you are likely

THE TARAHUMARA AND THE MENNONITES

The Copper Canyon area is home to the Tarahumara Indians, a shy and gentle people who live by farming and selling their handicrafts. Known for their long-distance running, some still live in caves and maintain their traditional lifestyles, although changes are evident.

The Mennonites, who settled around Cuauhtémoc in the early 1920s, are also farmers. They maintain their own lifestyle; their schools teach only their German dialect. Distinguishable by their pale complexion, the men wear blue dungarees, while the women sport wide-brimmed hats, long drab skirts and white stockings in the style of the 1830s.

to encounter some of the local Indians on your travels. Some of the caves they dwell in around Creel can also be visited. Another worthwhile trip is to the Basaseáchic Waterfall.

After Creel, the journey continues through an area of flat farmlands, grazing cattle and fruit orchards. The next stop, Cuauhtémoc, is worth another stopover to take a look at the Mennonite colony that lives in the surrounding area. You can visit a bookshop, school, cheese factory and perhaps a private home on a tour. The train arrives at its final destination in the evening. An overnight stay in Chihuahua will give you time to explore the town (*see pp116–17*).

(*see pp116–17*)

The dramatic peaks and gorges of Copper Canyon, Sierra Madre

A Tarahumara Indian weaves a basket in the traditional way

Trips on the Copper Canyon Railway can be arranged through:
Chihuahua: Turismo al Mar, Berna 2202.
Tel: (614) 410 9232, 416 5950.
www.copper-canyon.net.
For more information contact:
Ferrocarril Mexicano.
Tel: (614) 439 7212.
Freephone tel: (01 800) 367 3900.
www.ferromex.com.mx

Getting away from it all

Sanctuaries and nature reserves

In recent years, Mexico has become increasingly aware of the need to protect its wildlife and natural resources. As a result, a growing number of wildlife sanctuaries and biosphere reserves are being established. Ecotourism is now actively promoted, with a view to preserving nature and learning about indigenous cultures. In addition, it helps to provide local people with education and a means of livelihood.

Birdwatching

The Yucatán coast, being home to countless species, is a paradise for birdwatchers. The big attraction is the large colonies of pink flamingos at **Río Lagartos National Park** and the **Celestún Wildlife Refuge**. Río Lagartos, 45km (28 miles) east of Mérida, is a sanctuary for resident flamingos, in addition to herons, pelicans and

Flamingos seek sanctuary in the national parks of the Yucatán peninsula

numerous other species. The flamingos arrive there in April and lay their eggs in June. In September they leave for other estuaries, including Celestún, which is on the Gulf of Mexico coast west of Mérida. Celestún is a major winter migration site for pelicans and cormorants, herons, egrets and many other birds. **Contoy Island**, a wildlife preserve inhabited by 60 or so bird species, can be reached on a day trip from Cancún or Isla Mujeres. Pacific migratory bird habitats near Mazatlán are also the home of over 100 species, including the very rare tufted magpie jay. (*Enquire at your hotel for information on excursions.*)

Biosphere reserves

South of Tulum, in Quintana Roo, is the **Sian Ka'an Biosphere Reserve**, a large area of tropical rainforests, wetlands and marine habitats shared between 1,000 human residents (mainly Maya) and hundreds of species of plants and animals, some of them endangered. Coastal lagoons and mangrove swamps provide nesting sites for colonies of waterbirds. Every May sees the arrival of turtles, which lay their eggs on one of the last undeveloped stretches of coast in North America. (*All-day hikes, which include a three-hour boat trip, can be arranged in Cancún through Amigos de Sian Ka'an. Tel: (998) 848 1618. www.amigosdesiankaan.org*)

Calakmul is the largest of these reserves, extending from central

Sleek deer and stealthy jaguar, prey and predator: both are protected in sanctuaries

Campeche down to the Guatemalan border, where it links up with the **Maya Biosphere Reserve**. Rare orchids, howler monkeys, jaguars, ocelots and tapirs are some of the species found in its dense, ancient rainforests. Centred around the Mayan ruins of Bonampak, in Chiapas, is the recently established **Montes Azules Reserve**. (*This reserve is not easily accessible. Excursions can be arranged from Palenque.*)

Recently a biosphere reserve has been set up in the northern Gulf of California. Stretching from the mouth of the Colorado River down to Puerto Peñasco, it protects the area's rich marine ecology and restricts fishing.

Monarch butterfly sanctuary

Each year towards the end of October, a region in the highlands of Michoacán suddenly comes alive with the fluttering of black-and-orange wings. Millions of monarch butterflies, from the northern US and southern Canada, settle down for the winter in three main areas – Zitácuaro, Ocampo and Angangueo – located between Toluca and Morelia.

(It was only about 20 years ago that their place of migration was discovered.) They remain there for the winter, and then around the middle of April they return north, hundreds of millions of them.

They are part of an important balance in nature, contributing vitally to pollination, with the result that Michoacán is one of the richest states in Mexico in terms of flowers, fruit and plant life. The best time to see the monarchs is February or March. Several companies offer organised tours to the **El Rosario Sanctuary** near Angangueo. *Admission charge.*

Whale-watching

Baja California has one of Mexico's largest wildlife preserves for the protection of grey whales (*see pp126–7*). It covers several bays and lagoons near Guerrero Negro, halfway down the peninsula's Pacific coast. Whale-watching tours are becoming increasingly popular. (*Arrangements can be made to go whale-watching from Guerrero Negro.*)

Spa resorts

Mexico has numerous thermal springs, the majority in the central highlands. The Aztecs recognised their healing powers, and Emperor Moctezuma is known to have visited the spas at El Penon (close to the capital), Ixtapan de la Sal and Oaxtepec, among others.

Pleasant spa resorts have grown up around some of these, offering attractive accommodation, thermal baths and health treatments in soothing surroundings. Swimming, riding and other recreational activities are often at hand. The environs of Mexico City boast a number of fine establishments. Midweek visits will let you avoid the crowds.

The **Rancho La Puerta** health spa, located at the northern tip of Baja California, was voted the Top Spa Abroad by *Travel & Leisure* in 2000. The retreat, offering week-long stays of health, fitness and total relaxation, lies in a stunning 1,200ha (3,000-acre) nature reserve at the foot of mystic Mt Kuchumaa (1,175m/3,855ft high), in a region considered by many to have the finest year-round climate in North America. In operation since 1940, Rancho La Puerta offers a variety of individually unique Mexican cottages filled with quality folk art by top national artists for guests' enjoyment. A full range of treatments, activities and special diets is provided. Aldous Huxley, William F Buckley Jr, Madonna and Jodie Foster have been some of its celebrity guests.

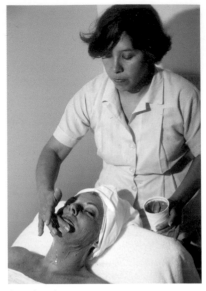

A mud mask

5km (3 miles) west of Tecate, Baja California. Tel: (665) 654 9155. www.rancholapuerta.com Reservations must be made in advance.

The quiet, whitewashed resort of Ixtapan de la Sal, about 130km (81 miles) southwest of Mexico City, has several hotels. Apart from the municipal spa, there is the privately run **Parque Los Trece Lagos** with Roman-style thermal baths and sulphurous pools for rheumatic ailments. Golf, tennis and bowling are just some of the other facilities.

An old favourite, with its feel of a bygone era, is **San José Purua**, located between Toluca and Morelia. This luxurious spa, recently renovated, is set in lush tropical gardens and perched on the rim of a deep gorge, with fantastic views of the mountains and a waterfall. A range of sports facilities complements its health-giving waters.

About 140km (87 miles) southeast of Puebla, the charming town of **Tehuacán** is famous for supplying most of the bottled water consumed in Mexico. The place has several hotels, and its thermal springs have been attracting people since pre-Hispanic times on account of their curative waters.

In the state of Querétaro, 18km (11 miles) north of San Juan del Río, is the picturesque spa resort of **Tequisquiapan**. Around its many thermal springs are several hotels with swimming pools, and golf and riding facilities are available in the vicinity.

The idyllic treatment tents at a hotel in Los Cabos

Shopping

For sheer variety of colourful products, Mexico is a shopper's delight. Its tradition of handicrafts, or artesanías, is very old indeed. Long before the Spanish Conquest, the indigenous people were producing pottery, wood carvings, woven goods and many crafts unique to each region.

The Spaniards introduced new elements of skill, design and function, and helped some Indian communities to develop their existing trades. The result of this marriage of Indian and Spanish talents is a number of top-quality goods of great flair and imagination. Handicrafts are available in shops and markets throughout Mexico. There are also many centres and shops where you can watch skilled craftsmen producing their wares.

Useful tips

Most regional handicrafts are also available in Mexico City but it can be more fun to browse around local shops and markets rather than shop in a busy capital which can, at times, be traumatic. In shops, the prices stand as marked, but in markets bargaining is expected as part of the game.

Although most local items look very attractive, appearances are sometimes deceptive. Always inspect your purchase, and remember that clothing may not always be colourfast or pre-shrunk.

Mexico has lovely semi-precious stones. Don't be persuaded to pay too much for them, and be wary of fake stones. When buying silver, look for the hallmark of .925. Don't confuse this real silver with the inexpensive, pretty jewellery called *alpaca*, which is only 25 per cent silver. Beware of so-called 'genuine' archaeological pieces on offer by the roadside. Good reproductions can be found in reputable shops (besides which, it is strictly forbidden to take genuine pieces out of the country).

Organised day trips invariably make a stop or two at handicraft centres where you are encouraged to spend. You may, of course, find all sorts of attractive items, but bear in mind that the goods may not be of the best quality and may be overpriced.

What to buy

The following list includes some of Mexico's best products and the regions of production:

Ceramics and pottery

Unglazed and highly glazed items.
Oaxaca, Tlaquepaque, Talavera, Puebla.

Gold filigreework

Oaxaca, Mérida.

Hammocks

Originally made from cotton, nowadays
often made from nylon.
Mérida, Veracruz.

Hand-blown glass

Glasses, vases, bowls, and dishes in
turquoise, green or red glass.
Tlaquepaque, Oaxaca, Mexico City.

Lacquerwork

Trays, bowls, boxes, gourds and other
items with encrusted decorations.
Pátzcuaro, Olinalá.

Onyx

Chess sets, ashtrays, boxes, bookends,
animal figures and decorative items.
Tecali.

Panama hats

Becal, Campeche, Mérida, Michoacán.

Semi-precious stones

Opals, topazes, aquamarines and
amethysts are predominant.
San Juan del Río, Querétaro, Durango.

Silverware and jewellery

Beautiful designs, often combining
modern and pre-Columbian motifs.
Taxco, Mexico City, Oaxaca, Mérida.

Textiles and traditional garments

Woven, brightly coloured woollen rugs:
Oaxaca, Mitla.
Serapes – a type of woollen blanket,
worn poncho-style, usually
multicoloured: *Saltillo.*
Rebozos – brightly coloured shawls: *San
Cristóbal de las Casas.*
Guayaberas – embroidered men's shirts
with tucks, usually white, but also in
other pale colours: *Mérida, Mexico City.*
Embroidered garments: *Oaxaca,
Mérida.*

Strut your stuff in a flashy sombrero, or just
keep cool under a Panama hat

Where to buy

You can pick up any number of pleasing souvenirs and gifts, functional or merely decorative, at very reasonable prices. It's often a real pleasure to wander around each town browsing small shops and markets, but it may be more practical to visit the well-set-up handicraft stores found in major towns. The following list displays a brief selection of some specialist shops.

Colourful Indian woven fabrics make lovely souvenirs

MEXICO CITY
Handicrafts
Bazar Sábado
Colourful market with quality handicrafts, Saturdays only.
Plaza San Jacieto, San Angel.
Centro de Artesanías La Ciudadela
Handicrafts from all over the country.
Balderas and Dondé.
Fonart
State-run chain of stores with attractively presented arts and crafts from all over Mexico.
Londres 136A,
Avenida Juárez 89 & Presidente Carranza 115, Coyoacán.
Palacio de las Máscaras
Specialises in fabulous masks from all over Mexico.
Allende 84. Tel: (55) 5529 2849.
The Green Door
Sells handicrafts, silver jewellery and high-quality pre-Columbian reproductions.
Cedro 8.
Tel: (55) 5591 0349.
Silver, gold and jewellery
Los Castillo
Outstanding quality and designs from an

established family firm from Taxco.
Amberes 41. Zona Rosa, Mexico City.
Tel: (55) 5511 6198.

OAXACA
Black pottery
Doña Rosa's Shop
Here you can watch the potters at work.
San Bartolo Coyotepec. 36km (22¹/2 miles) south.
Handicrafts
Fonart
Manuel M Bravo 116.
Tel: (951) 516 5764.
Casa de las Artesanías de Oaxaca
Matamoros 105.
Tel: (951) 516 5062.

Jewellery
Oro de Monte Albán
Adolfo C Gurríon. Tel:
(951) 516 4528.

San Miguel de Allende
Art galleries
Galería San Miguel
Plaza Principal 14.
Tel: (415) 152 0454.
Galería Sergio
Bustamante
Known for ceramic,
metal and papier-mâché
animal figures.
Mesones.
Handicrafts
Casa Maxwell
Canal 14.
Tel: (415) 152 0247.

TAXCO
Silverware and
jewellery
Emilia Castillo
Top-quality craftsman-
ship and outstanding
designs of silverware
and jewellery created
by the local Castillo
brothers.
Located in the Hotel
Emilia Castillo, Ruiz de
Alarcón 7.
Tel: (762) 622 3471.

TLAQUEPAQUE
Ceramics
Agustín Parra Diseño
Novohispano
Independencia 158.

Cerámica Guadalajara
Good selection of
ceramics and tiles.
Juárez 347.
Puente Viejo
Known for ceramics and
tinware.
Juárez 159.

Tlaquepaque is one of
Mexico's most famous
handicraft centres, with
an abundance of
colourful shops. You
should go for an
unhurried exploration of
the main shopping area, a
pedestrian zone west of
the plaza, and try to work
out some good bargains.

Shopping

Pottery and other collectables, little and large, at one of the handicrafts shops in Tlaquepaque

Indian markets

For centuries, since the Aztecs bought and sold at their *tianguis*, Mexico has had a tradition of markets, which continues to form an integral part of Mexican life, particularly for the indigenous population. Every town has its weekly or daily market, and old Indian markets in the smaller villages are ideal places at which to observe local ways.

Market day transforms overnight a small place into a sociable scene of bargain and banter. Indian women with long black plaits and numerous children mind their stalls, which are crammed with exotic fruits, fiery chillies, vivid flowers, rainbow-coloured rugs, pots and all manner of fascinating products. Local medicine men call out the benefits of strange potions and remedies for ailments. Haggling is standard practice.

Toluca's Friday market is perhaps the best known, though it is now too

A weaver's stall

huge. More enjoyable are the ones in Oaxaca (Saturday) and the neighbouring villages of Ocotlán (Friday) and Tlacolula (Sunday).

Deep in the highlands of Chiapas, the markets have another flavour. Of special interest are those of San Cristóbal de las Casas, and the Sunday market of nearby San Juan Chamula. These are particularly fascinating, being the gathering place of various Indian groups who come down from their surrounding hill communities, dressed in traditional costumes unique to each village, and speaking different languages.

Rich colours reflect the exuberant spirit that pervades local markets

Market stall in Tepoztlán

Entertainment

When it comes to entertainment in Mexico, the simplest forms are often the most satisfying. Just sitting in a bar or restaurant watching the action can be enjoyable. There is always plenty of music to liven things up, and no shortage of street life.

Bandstand concerts in town squares provide great entertainment at no cost. Nightclubs provide fun but at a noticeable cost! There are dance venues galore, especially in the resorts. In major cities there are concerts, opera and ballet, and unmissable performances of traditional song and dance.

Information on what's on in Mexico City can be found in a number of publications, including the daily English-language paper *The Herald Mexico*. *Time Out Mexico DF* is also available from newsagents. You will find that many hotels provide *Donde* and the annual *Travellers' Guide to Mexico*.

BARS

Hotel bars are popular evening meeting places for Mexicans. Many have live music, some have other entertainment. Many in coastal resorts feature loud tropical music and dancing.

Mexico City
Campanario Bar
Magnificent view of the *zócalo*.
Majestic Hotel, Madero 73. Tel: (55) 5521 8600.
Galería Plaza Bar
Lively lobby bar; jazz and a variety of music.
Hotel Galería Plaza, Hamburgo 195. Tel: (55) 5230 1717.
Jorongo Bar
Mariachis and other bands.
Sheraton María Isabel Hotel, Reforma 325. Tel: (55) 5442 5555.
Lobby Bar
Popular rendezvous spot.
Camino Real Hotel, Bar Blue Lounge, Mariano Escobedo 700. Tel: (55) 5263 8888.

Acapulco
Bar Terraza
Views of the beach.
Hyatt Regency Hotel, Costera Miguel Alemán 1. Tel: (744) 469 1234.

Cancun
Hard Rock Café
Boulevard Kukulcán, Centro Comercial 'Forum by the Sea'. Tel: (998) 529 881 8120.
Pat O'Brien's
Flamingo Plaza. Tel: (998) 883 0418.

Puerto Vallarta
El Nido Bar (Chez Elena)
Guitar music and beautiful sunset views.
Matamoros 520.
Tel: (322) 222 0161.
Friday López
Fiesta Americana Hotel, Km 2.5 Airport Rd.
Tel: (322) 322 42010.

CABARET

Many top hotels and some private establishments will offer a nightclub with a floor show, live music, and performances by well-known entertainers.

Mexico City
Area Bar and Terrace
at the Habita Hotel. Lounge music.
Av Presidente Mazaryk, Polanco. Tel: (55) 5282 3100 ext 460.
Barbarella
Nightclub featuring top entertainers.
Hotel Fiesta Americana, Reforma 80.
Tel: (55) 5705 1515.
Barracuda
Jazz, young couples and singles.
Nuevo Leon 4, Col Condesa.
Tel: (55) 5211 9480.

Mama Rumba
Cuban-style salsa club.
Querétaro 230.
Tel: (55) 5564 6920.
Rexo
Up-market scene.
Saltillo 1, Col Condesa.
Tel: (55) 5553 5337.
Sushi Groove
For those aged 30+.
Av Presidente Mazaryk 410, Polanco. Tel: (55) 5281 4412.
W Bar
Trendy, cosmopolitan.
At the W Hotel, Campos Eliseos 252, Polanco. Tel: (55) 9138 1800.

Bars and nightclubs start up, close down and reinvent themselves. So check before going.

CINEMA

Mexicans are avid film-goers and there are over 600 cinemas in Mexico City alone.

Mexico City
Cinética Nacional
Specialises in Mexican and international cultural films.
Avenida México-Coyoacán 389. Tel: (55) 1253 9390.
www.cinetecanacional.net

Classic films are occasionally presented at the Anglo-Mexican Cultural Institute, Antonio Caso 127, and the American Cultural Institute, Hamburgo 115.

CLASSICAL MUSIC, BALLET AND OPERA

Mexico City and major centres have some fine venues for concerts, opera and ballet.

Mexico City
Nezahualcoyotl Hall
Classical music, amid striking modern architecture.

Cinema billboard

Insurgentes Sur 3000.
Tel: (55) 5565 0709.

Ollin Yolitzli
One of Mexico's finest
concert halls.
Periférico Sur 1541.
Tel: (55) 5606 0016.

Palacio de Bellas Artes
Top venue for classical
music, opera and ballet.
Avenida Juárez and Eje
Central Lázaro Cárdenas.
Tel: (55) 5521 9251.

Guadalajara
Teatro Degollado
Home of the
Guadalajara Symphony
Orchestra. Concerts
and opera.
Plaza de la Liberación.
Tel: (33) 3613 1115.

Guanajuato
Teatro Juárez
Dance, drama and concerts.

Traditional Mexican dress as
worn by a dancer

Calle de Sopeña.
Tel: (473) 732 0183.

NIGHTCLUBS
The liveliest venues are
to be found at the beach
resorts, where the jet
set dance the night
away to deafening noise
levels. Trends change
with startling rapidity –
this year's hotspot may
well be next season's
history!

Acapulco
Los Albriges
La Costera 3308.
Tel: (744) 484 5902.

Alebrije
Av Costera Miguel
Aleman 3308. Tel: (744)
484 8025.

Baby 'O
Costera Miguel Alemán
and Horacio Nelson.
Tel: (744) 484 7474.

Disco Beach
Playa Condesa.
Tel: (744) 484 8230.

Nina's
Tropical and salsa.
Avenida Costera Miguel
Aleman 2909. Tel: (744)
484 2400.

Palladium
Carretera Escénica Fracc.
Guitarrón.
Tel: (744) 446 5490.

Premier
Salsa music.
Avenida Costera Miguel
Aleman. Tel: (744) 481
0114.

Cancun
Dady 'O
Blvd Kukulcán, Km 9.5.
Tel: (998) 883 3333.

La Boom
Blvd Kukulcán, Km 3.5.
Tel: (998) 883 1152.

Ixtapa
Carlos 'n Charlie's
Next to Hotel Posada
Real. Tel: (755) 553 0085.

Christine
Hotel Krystal, Blvd
Ixtapa. Tel: (755) 553
0456.

Puerto Vallarta
Andale
Olas Altas 425.
Tel: (322) 222 1054.

Christine
Hotel Krystal, Avenida de
las Garzas.
Tel: (322) 224 6990.

LOCAL ENTERTAINMENT
In most towns and
villages, life revolves
around the main square,
the *zócalo*. An enjoyable
time can be had sitting in

a bar watching the world go by. Sundays and feast days are particularly lively, when Mexican families are out *en masse* enjoying concerts or local dancing. Serenading is still practised by *estudiantinas*, the strolling musicians of Guanajuato who dress in traditional costume.

TRADITIONAL DANCE AND MUSIC

Mexico's great folk tradition manifests itself in colourful shows of regional songs and dances. An opportunity to see the superb Mexican national ballet company, Ballet Folklórico de Mexico, should not be missed. Many hotels, restaurants and special venues, regularly present 'Mexican Fiestas', which can be very entertaining evenings of song, dance and other performances.

Mexico City
Auditorio Nacional
Reforma and Campo Morte.
Tel: (55) 5280 9250.
www.auditorio.com.mx
Palacio de Bellas Artes
Dazzling presentation by

the Ballet Folklórico de México.
Avenida Juárez and Eje Central Lázaro Cárdenas.
Tel: (55) 5521 9251.
Wed evenings & Sun mornings.
Plaza Garibaldi
Famous square with many *mariachi* bands.
Plaza Santa Cecilia
Off Garibaldi Square.

Acapulco
Centro Internacional (Convention Centre)
Plaza Mexicana.
Tel: (744) 484 7152.
Marbella Plaza
Costera Miguel Alemán.

Cancún
Cancún Center
Paseo Kukulcán, Km 9.
Tel: (998) 881 0400;
www.cancuncenter.com
Hotel Gran Caribe Real
Paseo Kukulcán, Km 11.
Tel: (998) 881 5500.

Guadalajara
Plaza de los Mariachis
Home ground of the *mariachis*.
Teatro Degollado
Sunday morning performances by Grupo Folklórico.

Plaza de la Liberación.
Tel: (33) 3613 1115.

Puerto Vallarta
Camino Real Hotel
Playa Las Estacas.
Tel: (322) 221 5000.
Hotel Krystal Vallarta
Avenida de las Palmas.
Tel: (322) 224 0202.
Hotel Westin Regina
Paseo de la Marina Sur 205. Tel: (322) 226 1100.
La Iguana
Cárdenas 311 (between Constitución and Insurgentes).
Tel: (322) 228 0660.

Entertainment

Mexicans dance with flair and flamboyance

Fiestas

Fiesta – the very word conjures up images of music, laughter, dancing, feasting – and in Mexico fiestas are a way of life, an institution that verges on the sacred, an opportunity to set problems to one side and rejoice in the sheer vitality of it all. In all seasons, for all reasons; Mexicans sprinkle these celebrations through the calendar like confetti. Whether marking a religious occasion or a secular one, Mexicans do it with an abundance of flair and merriment.

Some fiestas go back to pagan times, relating to aspects of nature such as fertility or the harvest; these still contain ancient Indian customs and beliefs. Many others entered the picture with Christianity, and have a strongly Spanish flavour. Most combine elements of both belief systems, and any apparent contradictions between the two cultures are overlooked in the general bonhomie arising out of parading, dressing up, music-making – and not a little drinking, often rounded off, for good measure, with fireworks.

Each region cherishes its own style of celebrating, and this is proudly displayed in traditional music and dance. Jalisco's infectious *mariachi* rhythms, Veracruz's merry *sones*, the Yucatán's romantic *trovas* and graceful dancers, the Western-style sound of *norteño* music – all present a delightfully different facet of the Mexican character.

Some of the dances survived the culture shock of the Conquest, and continue to impress today's visitors as they undoubtedly did the first Spaniards. See, if you can, the *Venado* (stag dance) from Sonora in the north; the dance of the *Viejitos* (old men) from Michoacán; the *Panachos* (feather dance) from Oaxaca; or the *Quetzales*, with striking wheel-like headdresses, from Cuetsalán, Puebla. Whatever form it takes, each artistic expression personifies its region while contributing uniquely to Mexico's complex heritage.

Masks, costumes, dancing, bonhomie – all contribute to the spirit of a fiesta

Children

Mexicans are well known for their love of children, and you can be sure yours will be welcome and shown every consideration. Your best bet is to select a coastal resort with a good beach and pool, then spend your time in that area. There are many additional attractions for children such as horse or donkey rides along the beach, boat trips around the bay, sailing, fishing and mini-golf.

Touring with young children is not ideal. Heat, tummy upsets, delays and all sorts of problems can arise, besides which, major sights are often geared to adult interests. However, there is plenty in Mexico that will appeal to children: lakeside resorts, *hacienda*-type hotels in beautiful gardens, colourful markets and lively fiestas where people of all ages catch the *camaraderie*. The zoological gardens dotted about the country are also well worth visiting if you're in the vicinity. The following are some special attractions that children can enjoy, including world-class amusement parks.

MEXICO CITY AND SURROUNDINGS

Six Flags Mexico

Huge amusement park with up to eight 'theme' towns within. Over 50 spectacular rides and shows.
Picacho a Ajusco, south of the city. Tel: (55) 5728 7271. www.sixflags.com. Admission charge.

Papalote Museo del Niño

This state-of-the-art, totally interactive museum designed exclusively for children two years and up has four main areas of exhibits, with a touch of Mexican culture (*Our World, The Human Body, Conscience* and *Communication*), plus an IMAX theatre. *Section II of Chapultepec. Open: daily 10am–7pm (later during holidays). Tel: (55) 5237 1773; on weekends (01 800) 327 2727. www.papalote.org.mx. Admission charge.*

Zoológico de Chapultepec

Children's zoo, pony riding, miniature railway, boating on the lake. Amusement park and roller coaster. *Section 1 of Chapultepec Park. Tel: (55) 5553 6263. Open: Tue–Sun 9am–4.30pm. Free admission.*

ACAPULCO

Centro Internacional Para Convivencia Infantil (CICI)

See p79.

Papagayo Park
See p79.

GUADALAJARA
Parque Agua Azul
Large park with aviary, butterfly sanctuary, mini-train rides for children. *Calzada Independencia Sur & Avenida del Campesino. Tel: (33) 319 0328. Open: Tue–Sun 10am–6pm. Admission charge.*

Zoológico Guadalajara
Zoological gardens with animals in a natural setting. Large aviary. Tours by mini-trains. Adjoining is the Selva Mágica (Magic Jungle) Amusement Park. *Paseo del Zoológico 600. Tel: (33) 3674 4488. www.zooguadalajara.com.mx. Open: Wed–Sun 10am–5pm. Admission charge.*

Planetario Severo Díaz Galindo
Planetarium with hands-on exhibits. *Avenida Ricardo Flores Magón 599. Tel: (33) 3674 4106. Open: Tue–Sun 10am–6pm. Admission charge.*

PUEBLA
Zoológico Africam
Safari-type zoo with lots of animals. *21km (13 miles) southeast of Puebla. Tel: (222) 281 7000; www.africamsafari.com.mx. Open: daily 10am–5pm. Admission charge.*

TOLUCA
Zacango Zoo
Animals are free to wander about in lovely grounds that were formerly part of an old ranch. A special attraction, not just for children but adults as well, is the spacious walk-through aviary. *Off highway between Toluca & Ixtapan de la Sal. Tel: (722) 298 0634. Open: daily 10am–5pm. Admission charge.*

TUXTLA GUTIÉRREZ
Zoomat
One of the best zoological gardens in Mexico. All species are from Chiapas state and include jaguars, monkeys, a large tapir, brilliantly coloured tropical birds and an impressive reptile house. Magnificent setting in a natural jungle habitat, where the animals can roam around spacious enclosures. *Southeast of town, just off Libramiento Sur. Tel: (961) 614 4765. Open: Tue–Sun 8.30am–5.30pm. Admission charge.*

Snorkelling is a fun way to study marine life

Children

Sport and leisure

For those who wish to be active, there is plenty of choice. In major towns there is golf, tennis and horse riding, while beach resorts have facilities for all your favourite watersports (the Caribbean is a veritable diver's paradise). Charreadas, *bullfights and* jai alai *matches have that special Mexican flavour.*

SPECTATOR SPORTS

For information, tickets or guided tours, ask at your hotel, local tourist office or a travel agency.

Bullfights

Bullfighting is practically a national institution in Mexico, and most towns have a bullring. The main season is December to March, when the professionals perform in Mexico City's Plaza México, Calle A Rodín (*tel: (55) 5563 3961*). Bullfights (*corridas*) are held on Sundays, and normally start at 4pm.

Charreadas

Charreadas are Mexican-style rodeos, with displays of horsemanship by *charros* (cowboys) in dashing outfits. Girl riders, singers and *mariachi* bands combine to make this a very colourful show. In Mexico City, performances are held most Sunday mornings at the Lienzo del Charro (take the Picacho turning off the Periférico west of San Ángel), or the Rancho del Charro (just off Avenida Constituyentes, Chapultepec Park).

Football (soccer)

As in most of Latin America, the Mexicans are crazy about *futbol*. Matches are held in the Aztec Stadium, SA–Tlalpan 3465 (*tel: (55) 5617 8080*), and the Olympic Stadium, University City (*tel: (55) 5522 0491*).

Horse racing

Mexico City's Hipódromo de las Américas, off Avenida Manuel Ávila Camacho (*tel: (55) 5387 0685*), offers thoroughbred horse racing daily, except for Mondays and Wednesdays. There is a small admission fee.

Jai alai

This extremely fast and skilful game from the Basque country is a very popular sport in Mexico, arousing much excitement as well as fierce betting. Matches are held in the capital at the Frontón México, Plaza de la

República (*tel: (55) 5573 2888*), Tuesday to Saturday evenings at 7pm, and Sunday from 5pm.

PARTICIPATORY SPORTS

Ask your hotel or local tourist office for information on what's on offer.

Golf

Magnificent 18-hole golf courses feature at all the major tourist centres, where they are usually attached to hotels. Some resorts boast several courses. In and around major towns are elegant country golf clubs where visitors can play as the guest of a member, or sometimes on weekdays for a daily fee.

For information contact: Federación Mexicana de Golf, Av Insurgentes Sur, 1605 Piso 10, Torre Mural, Col San José, Insurgentes, México DF 03900. Tel: (55) 1084 2176. www.mexgolf.org

Hunting

Many regions of Mexico offer hunting, for both large and small game. There is also wing-shooting for ducks, geese, quail and doves. Always apply well in advance to book your hunt with a registered outfitter. It is best to rent equipment in Mexico and obtain a local hunting permit.

For information and the hunting season calendar write to the Secretaría de Agricultura y Recursos Hidraulicos, Dirección General de Flora y Fauna Silvestre, Av Revolución 1425, Col Tlacopac, Delegación Álvaro Obregón,

01040 México DF. Tel: (55) 5264 3309. Details on registered outfitters can be obtained from Claudia Ramsower, Mexico City. Tel: (55) 5390 1447.

Riding

Opportunities are endless, from ranch hotels and beach rides at resorts to organised expeditions in such exotic regions as the Copper Canyon or the highlands of Chiapas. Many rides take you through small villages, giving you a rare glimpse of local life.

Tennis

Tennis courts are attached to hotels in all popular resorts. Most cities and major towns have private tennis clubs where visitors can be invited to play by a member. In Puerto Vallarta, enthusiasts will enjoy the John Newcombe Tennis Centre next to the Plaza Vallarta Hotel.

Women horse-riders in traditional rodeo costumes

For information contact: Federación Mexicana de Tenis, Miguel Angel de Quevado 953, Coyoacán, México DF 04330. Tel: (55) 49 1956. www.fmt.com.mx

Boating and sailing

Mexico's coastal resorts, lakes and reservoirs offer ample opportunities for boating and sailing. All sorts of seagoing vessels can be hired at major resorts, ranging from canoes, catamarans and kayaks to sailing boats and large yachts.

Within range of Mexico City, the lakes of Tequesquitengo, Zempoala, Avandaro and Valsequillo Dam have boats for hire. Weather conditions are usually favourable during the winter months. Regattas are held in some resorts, including Acapulco, Cozumel, Ensenada, Manzanillo and Mazatlán.

Deep-sea fishing

Mexico's long Pacific coastline is renowned for its excellent deep-sea fishing, considered by many to rank among the best in the world. North Americans have been travelling down for years to fish in the Gulf of California. Main centres for fishing are Guaymas, Mazatlán, Manzanillo, Ensenada and Los Cabos, where charter boats and equipment are available. You can get a fishing licence through the local Fisheries Department office or through the captain of your chartered boat. Catch includes marlin, sailfish, swordfish, tuna and shark.

For information on fishing and permits contact: Secretaría de Pesca, Municipio Libre 269, Col Santa Cruz Atoyac, México DF. Tel: (55) 9183 1000.

Freshwater fishing

In recent years, Mexico has become known for its excellent black bass-fishing. Two of the best spots for this are the Vicente Guerrero Dam in Tamaulipas and the Comedero Dam in Sinaloa. In the central area, fishing is possible in the lakes of Zempoala, Valle de Bravo, Pátzcuaro, Chapala and many other lakes and reservoirs. Fishing tackle is available for hire in some centres.

Scuba diving and snorkelling

Mexico has developed into an idyllic destination for underwater enthusiasts. Many areas along its beautiful coastline offer excellent scuba diving, snorkelling and skin diving. Conditions are ideal in the Caribbean, where crystal-clear waters and coral reefs are the habitat of countless varieties of tropical fish. In the Yucatán Peninsula many lagoons and *cenotes* (*see p93*) provide superb diving experiences. Outstanding are the interlocking lagoons of Xel-Há, and the underground rivers and caves of Xcarat. At Akumal Bay, famous for skin diving, there is expert tuition available. Cozumel is renowned for its Palancar reef and the underwater caves of the Chancanab lagoon. El Garrafón in Isla Mujeres has an underwater coral garden.

The entire Sea of Cortés is a scuba-diver's paradise. You can arrange for scuba diving in virtually every town in Baja California, and choose from over 100 islands for a choice experience. Some of the best attractions include sighting hammerhead sharks, sea lions and giant stingrays, and exploring the Suwanee Reef and Las Animas Island.

Surfing

Pacific rollers here reach tremendous heights, which makes for world-class surfing beaches. The sport is gradually gaining in popularity, and enthusiasts are discovering new areas.

Some of the best beaches are around Puerto Escondido, Huatulco, Mazatlán and in Baja California. The island of Todos Santos, off Ensenada, is considered one of the top spots for surfing, though it should only be attempted by experts. Surfboards can be rented in major resorts.

White-water rafting

Veracruz is an excellent place for this exciting sport, with rafting activities in various rivers available for even novice enthusiasts. Rafting can also be done in San Luis Potosí, and in Acapulco's Papagayo River where even children as young as seven can enjoy the adventure of speeding down the river rapids.

Windsurfing

Windsurfing has caught on in a big way and is available in most resorts, with tuition if needed (just enquire on the beach). The sport is particularly popular in Cancún. Various hotels rent out equipment and offer tuition.

Pretty beaches invite watersports enthusiasts

Food and drink

Mexican cuisine is a combination of traditional Indian, Spanish, French and other European cuisines that were later introduced to the country. Its distinctive character can only be properly savoured in Mexico itself. Forget the myth that all Mexican food is hot and spicy. While hot chillies are used in certain recipes, they do not dominate the cuisine. A word to the wise, however: be cautious in trying the small bowls of sauce (salsa) that accompany many dishes. They may look similar, but can range from the bland to the blistering!

The basics

Maize and beans were cultivated in Mexico by early settlers. With their nutritional value, they continue to form the staple diet of many Mexicans today. No self-respecting Mexican meal is complete without its *tortillas*. Made from maize flour and formed into pancakes, they are eaten as a kind of bread with the meal. *Tortillas*, served with a portion of *refritos* (refried beans) and avocado-based *guacamole*, form the basis of numerous dishes. Stuffed, they become *tacos*. Topped with a sauce and baked, they are called *enchiladas*. *Quesadillas, tostadas, burritos* and *chilaquiles* are variants of *tortilla*-based dishes.

Regional cooking

Each region has its own style and specialities. Oaxaca and Puebla (of *mole poblano* fame) are noted for good traditional cooking. The Yucatán offers tasty pork, fiery chillies and delicately flavoured dishes steamed in banana leaves. The best beef comes mostly from the cattle ranches of Sonora, while Monterrey is known for *cabrito* (roast kid).

Coastal resorts offer a great variety of seafood, with Veracruz and Campeche, on the Gulf of Mexico, renowned for the quality of their fish. A popular dish is *ceviche*, fish marinated in lime juice.

When the Spanish conquistadores arrived, they discovered delicious and wholesome new foods native to Mexico. Among these were sweetcorn and beans (which the Indians had long cultivated), peanuts, tomatoes, chillies, pumpkins, courgettes, avocados, pineapples, turkey, and vanilla, spices and cacao (chocolate was known to be a favourite drink of the Aztec emperor Moctezuma).

All these foodstuffs were introduced into Europe, and are now taken for granted as part of our normal diet. Maize has become an important crop worldwide, and beans are valued in all cuisines for their high-quality protein and fibre.

Eating out

Eating out in Mexico is fun. The country is noted for its long luncheons, which can last from 2pm till well past sundown. You can eat as little or as much as you like without feeling pressurised. Many restaurants offer international as well as Mexican dishes, the latter generally being cheaper. Mexico City and major towns offer a wide selection, ranging from the ultra-sophisticated to traditional Mexican.

Although Mexicans prefer meat-based dishes, vegetarians are also generally well catered for, with plenty of dishes using beans and other pulses, and seafood options too for those who eat fish. Mexican vegetarian dishes are seldom as bland as those you can find in some other cuisines.

The following are likely to be included in a typical menu:
Ceviche: fish marinated in lime juice.
Chiles rellenos: green peppers stuffed with spicy minced beef or cheese.
Huevos rancheros: fried eggs with tomato sauce atop *tortillas* spread with refried beans.
Mole poblano: turkey or chicken with rich sauce.
Sopa de tortilla: broth with strips of *tortilla*, chicken and avocado.
Tacos de pollo: chicken-filled *tortillas*.
Tamales: steamed maize husks filled with meat.

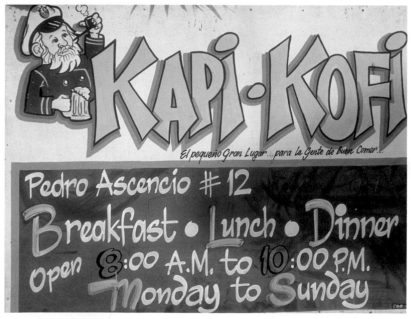

Dine at the captain's table in Zihuatanejo

Mexican buffet breakfasts

Breakfast in a Mexican hotel is in a category of its own. First, there is the ambience (business meetings are regularly conducted over breakfast), then there is the buffet, which is offered by most top-class hotels.

The array of dishes is nothing short of splendid. Apart from the whole range of tropical fruits and juices, there are all sorts of hot dishes with tempting accompaniments. The staff will always explain them to you if you ask, or even if you don't! For something hot to drink, there's the familiar choice of coffee, tea and chocolate. (Coffee, once poor in quality, has greatly improved in recent years.) Some popular dishes are *huevos revueltos a la mexicana* (scrambled eggs with chopped tomato, onion and chilli), *huevos rancheros* (fried eggs with a spicy tomato sauce), and *chilaquiles* (*tortillas* in a sauce). You will even have the option of a steak. A hearty Mexican breakfast certainly goes a long way!

Fruits

The selection of tropical fruits in Mexico is vast. Year round you can enjoy mangoes, pineapples, papayas, guavas, melons, water-melons, *tuna* (cactus fruit), oranges, apples and (instead of lemon) limes – which give that special Mexican flavour to everything. Breakfast is a good time to enjoy them.

Drinks and beverages

Mexico's foremost alcoholic beverage, *tequila*, needs no introduction. This plant-based spirit is world-famous, and its Margarita and Tequila Sunrise cocktails are known in bars everywhere. The traditional way to drink *tequila* is to take it neat with a pinch of salt and suck of a lime. An unusual but delicious concoction is *tequila*, lime juice and Maggi (a brand-name savoury liquid seasoning). Lesser known, but equally potent, is *mezcal*, and the low-alcohol *pulque*, derived from the maguey plant (*see pp168–9*).

Rum, another product of Mexico, is used in many cocktails. The famous Cuba Libre (rum and Coke) and Planter's Punch are popular rum based drinks. Kahlua is a pleasant coffee-flavour liqueur.

Many varieties of beer are produced in Mexico, mainly in the north and the

Street vendors offer tempting arrays of fresh fruit, but always peel it before eating

Yucatán, and they perfectly complement the national cuisine. Whether *clara* (light) or *oscura* (dark), they are customarily served chilled. Some of the most popular brands are Superior, Bohemia, Corona, Dos Equis and Carta Blanca.

Although a wine producer, Mexico is not a wine-drinking country as such. However, the growth of the industry has greatly improved the quality of wines in recent years. Wine-growing areas are in Baja California and central Mexico. Calafia wine from Baja California is a good table wine.

The so-called *café americano* tends to be weak, but many places now offer espresso. An alternative is *café de olla* (coffee with cinnamon), served in tiny earthenware cups. Mexicans drink a lot of tea. Try it with lime, as they do.

Be careful

To avoid holiday tummy (called *turista*, Moctezuma's Revenge or the Toltec Two-Step), take sensible precautions. Steer clear of salads, except in American-style hotels in major resorts, and always peel fruit. Be careful of pork in tropical locations. Do not drink tap water and always avoid unpasteurised milk. Also, it is wise to resist the temptation of buying food from roadside stalls. (*See* Health, *p183*.)

Margarita

3 parts tequila
1 part Triple Sec (or Cointreau)
2 parts lime juice
Shake it with ice or mix it in a blender. Then strain it into cocktail glasses whose rims have been dipped in lime juice and frosted with salt.

Food and drink

An exotic array of fruits and vegetables in a town market

Tequila, mezcal and pulque

The worm in the *mezcal* bottle

the many distilleries in the area might help unravel the mysteries of the legendary liquor. After your tequila tasting, all will become clear!

Basically, the centre of the maguey is cut out, roasted and mashed. This is then placed into fermenting barrels to

Vast plantations of the agave plant are a familiar sight in Mexico. From the 400 or so existing species, a few are used for the production of three native liquors – *tequila*, *mezcal* and *pulque* – each of which is made from a different variety. *Tequila* and *mezcal* are intoxicants produced by a process of fermentation followed by distillation, while *pulque* is made by fermentation alone, and is low in alcohol content.

Tequila is, in fact, a high-quality variant of *mezcal*. It is produced only from the blue maguey, or the *Agave tequilana*, which grows around the towns of Tequila and Tepatitlán, near Guadalajara, Jalisco. A visit to one of

which yeast is added. The fermented mash is then distilled twice. Colourless *tequila* is bottled direct from the barrel, while aged *tequila* acquires a golden colour. *Conmemorativo* is a top-quality *tequila* that has aged for seven years.

Mezcal-producing areas are located in the southeast, southwest and northern regions of Mexico. Unlike *tequila*, which has acquired international status, *mezcal* is mainly consumed locally, and is exported on a limited basis. It is quite usual to find a worm (*gusano de maguey*) in the bottom of the bottle. If this does not appeal, stick to *tequila*.

Pulque is an ancient type of nectar dating back to long before the arrival of the Spaniards. It is served in *pulquerías*, where strangers are not too welcome and women are rarely seen.

You are bound to see fields of agave growing in Mexico

Beachfront dining

Where to eat

In a country such as Mexico that caters to foreign visitors with such enthusiasm, the choice of places to eat is quite extensive, even in small to mid-sized towns! In major centres, restaurants and local eateries exist in all price categories.

In the listings below, the star symbols indicate the typical cost for a meal for two, including drinks. Service charges are rarely included, and a tip of 10–15 per cent should be added on top.

★	200 pesos and under
★★	200–400 pesos
★★★	400–500 pesos
★★★★	500 pesos and up.

MEXICO CITY
International
Cicero-Centenario ★★★★
Gourmet Mexican fare with international flare: another branch in the historic centre.
Londres 195, Zona Rosa. Tel: (55) 5533 3800.

Estoril ★★★★
Elegant restaurant, known for its excellent cuisine, housed in an attractive mansion in the Polanco district. Patronised by the smart set.
Alejandro Dumas 24, Polanco. Tel: (55) 5280 1107.

Hacienda de los Morales ★★★★
Magnificent setting in 17th-century *hacienda*.
Vázquez de Mella 525. Tel: (55) 5096 3054.

San Angel Inn ★★★★
Located 45 minutes south of the centre, but worth the journey for its setting in a restored 18th-century *hacienda*.
Diego Rivera 50, corner of Altavista and San Angel. Tel: (55) 5616 1402.

European
Au Pied de Cochon ★★
Mexican outpost of the venerable Parisian favourite, housed in the Intercontinental Hotel.
Campos Eliseos 218. Tel: (55) 5327 7700.

Bellini ★★★★
Rotating restaurant on top of the World Trade Center. Great views of the city. Italian/ international cuisine.
Montecitos 38, alongside Avenida Insurgentes. Tel: (55) 5628 8305.

Meson del Cid ★★★

Its attractive setting and authentic Spanish dishes with special suckling pig ceremony draw large crowds.
Humboldt 61.
Tel: (55) 5521 6998.

Mexican

Fonda el Refugio ★★

Famous for classic dishes (even Mexicans queue to get a table).
Liverpool 166.
Tel: (55) 5525 8128.

Izote de Patricia Quintana ★★★★

Old recipes given new twist by one of the city's star chefs.
Presidente Masaryk 513.
Tel: (55) 5280 1671.

La Casa de las Sirenas ★★★

21st-century food in 17th-century building, combining gastronomy with romance.
Republica de Guatemala 32. Tel: (55) 5704 3225.

La Valentina ★★★★

Mexican *haute cuisine*. Live *mariachi* music at lunchtime, other live entertainment in the evenings.
Avenida Insurgentes 1854.
Tel: (55) 5282 2656.

Los Girasoles ★★

Good location downtown, with lively ambience. Succulent marrowbone is one of the restaurant's special delicacies.
Calle de Tacuba, Plaza Manuel Tolsa.
Tel: (55) 5510 0630.

Sea food restaurants

Restaurant Danubio ★★★

Seafood favourite in the historical centre since 1936.
Uruguay 3.
Tel: (55) 5512 0912.
www.danubio.com

ACAPULCO

Beto's ★★

Two adjoining beach restaurants.
Costera Miguel Alemán.
Tel: (744) 484 0473.

El Amigo Manuel ★★

Authentic Mexican seafood specialist, not pricey so always packed.
Juárez 31. Tel: (744) 483 6981.

CANCÚN

La Habichuela ★★★

Named for the house special of bean soup, this place has a beautiful Mayan-style courtyard dining area.
Margaritas 25. Tel: (998) 884 3158.

MÉRIDA

La Misión de Fray Diego ★★

Mayan specialities in excellent hotel restaurant.
Calle 61 no 524.
Tel: (999) 924 1111.

OAXACA

Asador Vasco ★★

Spanish dishes. A very attractive location overlooking the *zócalo*.
Portal de Flores 10A, 1st Fl. Tel: (951) 514 4755.

PUERTO VALLARTA

Daiquiri Dick's ★★

This old favourite right on the beach serves Mexican and Californian dishes.
Olas Altas, Los Muertos Beach.
Tel: (322) 222 0566.

El Arrayan ★★★

Winning prizes for the best *tacos* in town, El Arrayan serves authentic local dishes.
Allende 344. Tel: (322) 222 7195.

Hotels and accommodation

Mexico has accommodation to suit all types of clientele, from the budget traveller to the corporate businessman. Ultra-modern, high-rise hotels in coastal resorts contrast with charming colonial-style accommodation in the interior of the country.

Although government ratings were abolished in 1993, hotels continue to use a rating system as follows: Categoría Especial, or CEsp (special properties with distinctive features); Gran Turismo or GT (establishments with amenities of exceptionally high quality); 5-star down to 1-star; Categoría Económica (or budget); and Sin Categoría (no category). This rating system is only a guideline, based primarily on amenities offered.

The following approximate double-room rates are given in local currency, excluding the 10–15 per cent IVA (VAT) and 2 per cent lodging tax now charged in some states. These are subject to change and higher seasonal tariffs in coastal resorts (mid-December to mid-April). Room rates can be lower when part of a package deal. Some hotels in Mexico City offer lower weekend rates.

Categoría Especial over P1,500
Gran Turismo P1,300–1,500
5-star P1,000–1,300
4-star P900–1,000
3-star P600–900
2-star P500–600
1-star P300–500.

Top de-luxe hotels in Mexico usually adhere to the highest worldwide standards of service, while establishments in the medium category provide comfort, coupled with a more personal atmosphere. Rooms are generally spacious and attractively decorated. In the upper categories you can expect to find a colour TV, minibar, private bathroom, all the usual facilities and sometimes the convenience of your own safety deposit box.

Useful tips

Drink purified bottled water, even if the tap water is said to be drinkable. Be warned about the high cost of long-distance telephone calls from your hotel room. Avoid an unpleasant surprise by using a phone box instead, or, better still, reverse the charges!

Major hotel chains
(in Mexico City)

(01 800 numbers are freephone in Mexico)

Aristos Hotels *Tel: (55) 5200 0112/ (01 800) 9010 200.*

Best Western *Tel: (55) 9149 3000/ (01 800) 528 1234.*

Camino Real *Tel: (55) 5263 8888.*

Club Royal Maeva *Tel: (55) 5284 0394.*

Day's Inn *Tel: (01 800) 325 2525.*

Fiesta Americana *Tel: (55) 2581 1500.*

Four Seasons *Tel: (55) 5230 1818/ (01 800) 906 7500.*

Hilton *Tel: (55) 5133 0500*

Holiday Inn *Tel: (55) 5130 5130/ (01 800) 007 9900.*

Howard Johnson *Tel: (01 800) 932 4658.*

Hyatt International *Tel: (55) 9138 1234.*

Krystal Hotels *Tel: (55) 5261 7777/(01 800) 005 0000.*

Marriott *Tel: (55) 5599 000/(01 800) 900 8800.*

Meliá *Tel: (55) 5128 5000/ (01 800) 901 7100.*

Mision Hotels *Tel: (55) 5209 1700.*

Presidente Inter-Continental *Tel: (55) 5327 7700/(01 800) 007 9900.*

Quality Inn (Calinda) *Tel: (55) 1085 9500/(01 800) 900 0000.*

Radisson *Tel: (55) 5627 0220.*

Sheraton *Tel: (55) 5130 5252/ (01 800) 470 7070.*

Starwood Luxury Collection *Tel: (55) 5130 5300/(01 800) 325 3589.*

Hotels and accommodation

The Acapulco Princess is one of Acapulco's grandest hotels

Business hotels

The business person is well catered for in Mexico City and other major destinations such as Acapulco, Cancún, Guadalajara and Monterrey. The larger hotels have executive suites and facilities for meetings and conventions. They also offer fax, secretarial, translating and many other professional services.

The **Nikko, J.W. Marriott, Inter-Continental Presidente, Camino Real** and **María Isabel Sheraton** are among the top business hotels in Mexico City, and can host conventions both large and small, supplying all the necessary equipment. The smaller **Clarion Reforma Suites** cater specially for business people, claiming to be able to meet virtually any requirements, from technical equipment to multilingual interpreting services and private transport. Most rooms are de-luxe suites, some complete with jacuzzi.

Beach hotels

Magnificent hotels line the shores of Mexico's popular resorts. High-rise buildings are much in evidence, but some resorts such as Cancún feature more innovative architecture. The majority of hotels are on the beach, and set in tropical gardens, with one or more swimming pools to supplement what nature provides. These are most attractively designed and offer all the comforts of beach and poolside

Character in abundance at the Hotel San Diego in Guanajuato

sunloungers, cocktail service, swim-up bars and blissfully warm water.

Resort complexes
A number of hotels are virtually resorts in themselves. Two outstanding examples are to be found in Acapulco: the world-famous **Las Brisas**, with its bungalows, individual swimming pools and views of Acapulco Bay, and the pyramid-shaped **Acapulco Princess**. Hotel complexes continue to spring up along Mexico's coastlines, each with its own individual character. Dotted along the beautiful, wild stretch of coast between Puerto Vallarta and Manzanillo, known as the Costa de Oro (Gold Coast), are a number of contrasting hotels, including **Las Hadas**, a spectacular Arabian Nights-type fantasy featured in the film *10*, the charming, rustic **Careyes**, **Los Angeles Locos** (The Crazy Angels) and **Las Alamandas**, creation of Isabel Goldsmith.

Colonial-style hotels
In the interior of the country are a number of picturesque hotels that were *haciendas* (ranch houses) back in colonial times. Set in beautiful surroundings, they will offer swimming, tennis, riding and other pastimes. Weekends tend to be busy with Mexican families. The **Hacienda Vista Hermosa**, **Hacienda Cocoyoc**, **Mansión Galindo**, **Antigua Hacienda de Galindo**, **Hacienda Juríca** and **Hotel San Miguel Reglas** are among the most magnificent. (*Also see pp176–7.*)

Condominiums and service flats
Major coastal resorts such as Acapulco, Puerto Vallarta and Cancún have large, modern condominiums (condos) for rent. Most are right on the beach and consist of large, self-contained apartments, fully furnished and equipped. Some can be booked through rental agencies in the capital.

Youth hostels
Only a handful of youth hostels are to be found, spread over the country. Information can be obtained from the Dirección de Atención a la Juventud. *Tel: (55) 5348 0023.*

Camping
Campsites are widespread and range from basic to luxurious, the latter usually aimed at the motor-home owner. Private individuals will often let people camp on their land, and it is also acceptable to camp on beaches, which are public property, although they are dangerous places to stay (*see p181*).

Prices (double room per night)
Business hotels year-round US$150–220.
Beach hotels high season US$180–350 (rates are generally reduced by about 30 per cent in the low season – around mid-April to mid-December).
Resort complexes high season US$200–300 (see above for low-season reductions).
Colonial-style hotels year-round US$100–200.
Youth hostels per person US$40–70.
Note: prices are given in dollars as these are often accepted in Mexico.

Haciendas

After the Conquest, the Spaniards developed agriculture and mining, acquiring ever more land and establishing large estates, called *haciendas*. These estates were concentrated in certain regions: in the mining areas of the central highlands and the north, in the cattle regions of the dry central plains, Chiapas and Veracruz, the sugar cane areas around the humid Gulf of Mexico and Morelos, the *henequen* region of the Yucatán, the coffee- and tobacco-growing areas of Veracruz and the cotton plantations in Coahuila.

Under the Spanish system of land grants, the owner was absolute ruler over his Indian workers who lived on the estate and were completely beholden to him. For 300 years there was much growth and prosperity for the Spaniards. Although they lost their rule in 1821, the *hacienda* system has not died out.

This beautiful *hacienda* was the home of the Mexican revolutionary leader Antonio López de Santa Ana

Hacienda del Pacifico, Ensenada

Great changes were brought about by the 1910–20 Revolution. Many *haciendas* were burnt down or pillaged. Land reforms gave Indians the right to own their own land. Some huge estates remained under one ownership, particularly in Chihuahua, but many were abandoned and fell into decay. Today, however, many of these former *haciendas* live and breathe again, converted into superb hotels in beautiful surroundings. With their lovely old rooms and graceful arcaded Spanish-style courtyards, they offer ideal accommodation for the discerning traveller with an appreciation of history.

Many *haciendas* are within the range of Mexico City. The magnificent Haciendas Vista Hermosa (tel: (734) 345 5382) and Cocoyoc (tel: (735) 356 1212), near Cuernavaca, inspire particular historical interest as former properties of the great conquistador Hernán Cortés. In San Miguel de Allende, there are: Hacienda Taboada (*tel: (415) 152 9250*) and Hacienda El Santuario (*tel: (415) 185 2036*). It doesn't take too much effort to conjure up images of famous figures of the past . . .

On business

Mexico is a member of the OECD (Organisation for Economic Cooperation and Development) and offers a wide variety of business opportunities. Its commercial relationships with countries all over the world keep growing at a steady pace.

Business etiquette

Doing business in Mexico is a very personal matter. It is important to deal directly with the top person and to get on friendly terms. Meetings should start with general pleasantries before progressing to business matters. Entertaining plays an important role and working breakfasts are a popular way of mixing business with pleasure. Formal attire – suit and tie for men – should be worn at all times in the cities.

Once back in your own country, it is important to maintain personal contact. One phone call can be far more effective than writing.

Business travel

Depending on the nature of your business, you may require a visa for Mexico. Check with your local consulate before departure. Travel is straightforward, with all main centres linked by regular air services or highways. Private air transport or car hire is also available.

Communications

Mexico offers international courier services (DHL, Federal Express, UPS), as well as local alternatives such as Estafeta and Mexpost. Telephone numbers and area codes changed recently; check your information is up to date. Public and private faxes can be expected in most places. The *Herald Mexico* provides useful information in English.

Conference and exhibition facilities

Major venues for large conferences and exhibitions are:

MEXICO CITY

Auditorio Nacional, Paseo de la Reforma 50, Bosque de Chapultepec. *Tel: (55) 5280 9250/7844.*

Exhibimex, Avenida Cuauhtémoc s/n, Esq Antonio M Anza. *Tel: (55) 5271 6734.*

Hotel Camino Real, Mariano Escobed 700. *Tel: (55) 5263 8888.*

Hotel InterContinental Presidente, Campos Eliseos. *Tel: (55) 5327 7700.* Hotel J.W. Marriott, Campos Eliseos. *Tel: (55) 5999 0000.* Hotel María Isabel Sheraton, Reforma 325. *Tel: (55) 5442 5555.* Hotel Nikko, Campos Eliseos 204. *Tel: (55) 5283 8700.*

ACAPULCO

Centro Internacional Acapulco, the largest convention centre in the country(Plaza Mexicana, *tel: (744) 434 0159).* Another is The Fairmont Acapulco Princess (Playa Revolcadero, *freephone tel: (01 800) 090 9900/746 9100).*

CANCÚN

Cancún Centre and Exhibition Hall, Kukulcán Blvd, Km 9. *Tel: (998) 881 0400.*

GUADALAJARA

Quinta Real, Avenida México 2727, at López Mateos Sur. *Tel: (33) 3669 0600.*

QUERETARO

Hotel Fiesta Americana, Hacienda Galindo, Carr Amealco, Km 5.5 off México-Querétaro Highway. *Tel: (427) 271 8200.*

The British Chamber of Commerce, Río de la Plata 30, Mexico City, *tel: (55) 5256 0901. www.britchamexico.com.* This office offers assistance to business people and can provide modern office and conference facilities. Assistance may also be offered by the British Embassy, Commercial Affairs, Río Lerma 71, Mexico City. *Tel: (55) 5242 8500; www.embajadabritanica.com.mx. Email: commsec@embajadabritanica.com.mx*

The Acapulco convention centre, sleek and modern with all facilities

Practical guide

Arriving

Travellers from the UK, Australia, New Zealand, Canada and South Africa will need a Tourist Card, valid for 90 days (but can be validated for 180 days on request). A passport, valid for six months, is also required, except for Canadian and US visitors who need not have passports as long as they hold proof of citizenship (birth certificate or voter registration card).

A customs declaration form, presented on board the aircraft or at customs, must also be handed in on arrival. There are no health requirements. Visitors who require visas should apply in their country of residence.

By air

Mexico City is well served by frequent flights from Europe, the US and other destinations. There are also direct flights from the US and Canada to other major centres, with an increasing number of flights from Europe to tourist resorts such as Cancún and Puerto Vallarta.

Taxis queue outside the airport building, and tickets are sold at special booths for a set price, according to zone. Always ignore touts offering private transport.

By bus

There are first-rate bus services from the main US entry points and from within the country to destinations all over Mexico. Just bear in mind the long distances to be covered.

By car

Travellers arriving by car must have a valid driving licence; a 90-day permit for the driver of the vehicle (from Mexican customs at the point of entry); a fully comprehensive insurance policy (also obtainable at the border); proof of ownership of the vehicle or a letter of authorisation from the owner.

An international driving licence is also recommended for Europeans. Note that you will not be permitted to leave the country without your car (on entry you must sign an affidavit stating that you will not sell the car in Mexico, and leave photocopies of proof of ownership, driver's licence and credit card).

By rail

Rail travel is the cheapest but also the slowest form of transport in Mexico, and often subject to delays. The *Thomas Cook Overseas Timetable*, published bi-monthly, will help you plan a railway journey to, from and around Mexico. It is available in the UK from some railway stations, at any branch of Thomas Cook or by phone at *01733 416477*.

Camping

Campsites and trailer parks are found in many parts of the country, including some of the national parks. In some coastal areas you can rent a hammock and sleep under a *palapa* (open thatched-roof hut). Never camp overnight on the beach or in any spot other than a designated site.

Children

On domestic flights, an adult is entitled to travel with one infant (under two years old) not occupying a seat. Children up to 12 years must pay the child's fare. On long-distance buses, children pay full fare if occupying a seat. However, there are usually reductions for rail travel.

Many hotels have rooms for three people, or can provide an extra bed for a child. Some can also provide nanny services on request. Some restaurants offer children's portions at lower prices.

Climate

See p28.

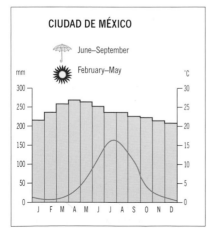

CIUDAD DE MÉXICO

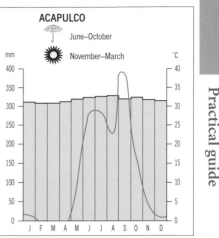

ACAPULCO

WEATHER CONVERSION CHART

25.4mm = 1 inch
$°F = 1.8 × °C + 32$

Clothing

See p28.

Conversion tables

See p183.

Crime

As in any other country, watch your belongings in crowded areas and do not leave them unattended. Be extra-vigilant on local transport in Mexico City. Deposit valuables in the hotel safe. Stick to central and well-lit areas when walking in the evenings. Never leave valuables visible inside your vehicle.

Customs regulations

Visitors entering Mexico are allowed 3 litres (5 1/4 pt) of wine or spirits, 400 cigarettes or 50 cigars, one camcorder and one regular camera (and up to 12 rolls of film), gifts not exceeding a total of US$300.

A completed Customs Declaration Form must be handed in to customs and a button pressed. Then a red light will signal a search that will be made, while a green light allows you to pass through without inspection. No drugs, weapons or pornography may be brought in, and no pre-Columbian art or artefacts may be taken out.

Driving

Car rental requirements are a valid driving licence (an international driving licence is recommended), a passport and a driver over 25. Insurance is arranged through the hire company. Avoid driving at night. *Angeles Verdes* (Green Angels) patrol

the highways to offer free assistance at all times. Driving is on the right side of the road.

Drugs

Trafficking in or being in possession of narcotics is a federal offence, and penalties are extremely severe.

Electricity

Most of Mexico operates on 110 volts AC, 60 cycles. From Europe you need to bring an adaptor for 2-pin flat plugs.

Embassies and Consulates

The following are all in Mexico City:
Australia Ruben Dario 55, Colonia Polanco. *Tel: (55) 1101 2200.*
Canada Schiller 529.
Tel: (55) 5724 7900.
UK Rio Lerma 71. *Tel: (55) 5242 8500.*
US Reforma 305 (next to Hotel

The roads, especially in Mexico City, are well maintained

Maria Isabel Sheraton and Towers).
Tel: (55) 5080 2000.
Consulates are also based in other major towns. The UK has consuls in Guadalajara, Cancún, Monterrrey and Acapulco.

Emergency telephone numbers
Ambulance *065*
Fire *068*
Police *060*
Cruz Roja (Red Cross) *065*
American British Cowdray Hospital (ABC), for emergencies *(55) 5230 8000.*

Health
Strict food and water hygiene will help avoid problems with diarrhoea, often known as *turista*. Make sure food has been properly washed and prepared; drink only bottled, sterilised water. If travelling inland or off the beaten track, consider taking anti-malarial tablets. AIDS is prevalent.

Insurance
Travellers to Mexico should take out full comprehensive insurance to cover illness, loss or theft and flight cancellation. Report any loss or theft to the police to get the necessary written confirmation for insurance claims.

Media
The only English-language newspaper in Mexico is the *Mexico Herald*, which is a daily Mexico supplement of the *Miami Herald*.

CONVERSION TABLE

FROM	TO	MULTIPLY BY
Inches	Centimetres	2.54
Feet	Metres	0.3048
Yards	Metres	0.9144
Miles	Kilometres	1.6090
Acres	Hectares	0.4047
Gallons	Litres	4.5460
Ounces	Grams	28.35
Pounds	Grams	453.6
Pounds	Kilograms	0.4536
Tons	Tonnes	1.0160

To convert back, for example from centimetres to inches, divide by the number in the third column.

MEN'S SUITS

UK	36	38	40	42	44	46	48
Rest of Europe	46	48	50	52	54	56	58
USA	36	38	40	42	44	46	48

DRESS SIZES

UK	8	10	12	14	16	18
France	36	38	40	42	44	46
Italy	38	40	42	44	46	48
Rest of Europe	34	36	38	40	42	44
USA	6	8	10	12	14	16

MEN'S SHIRTS

UK	14	14.5	15	15.5	16	16.5	17
Rest of Europe	36	37	38	39/40	41	42	43
USA	14	14.5	15	15.5	16	16.5	17

MEN'S SHOES

UK	7	7.5	8.5	9.5	10.5	11
Rest of Europe	41	42	43	44	45	46
USA	8	8.5	9.5	10.5	11.5	12

WOMEN'S SHOES

UK	4.5	5	5.5	6	6.5	7
Rest of Europe	38	38	39	39	40	41
USA	6	6.5	7	7.5	8	8.5

Language

While English is quite widely spoken in tourist resorts, some knowledge of Spanish goes down well and is needed if travelling off the beaten track.

PRONUNCIATION

a as in p**a**lm

e as in l**a**te or g**e**t

i as in f**ee**t

o as in p**o**t

u as in p**u**ll

y as in f**ee**t.

c like **s** before the letters **e** and **i**, otherwise like **k**

ch as in **ch**urch

g like **h** as in **h**at before **e** and

i, otherwise as in **g**o

h is always silent

j like **h** in **h**a

ll usually like **y** in **y**et

ñ like **ni** in o**ni**on

qu like **k**

r is rolled

s is generally as in **s**it

x usually as in ta**x**i, before a consonant, like **s** in **s**it, in Indian words, often like the **ch** in lo**ch**.

NUMBERS

0	cero	7	siete	14	catorce	30	treinta
1	uno	8	ocho	15	quince	40	cuarenta
2	dos	9	nueve	16	dieciseis	50	cincuenta
3	tres	10	diez	17	diecisiete	100	cien
4	cuatro	11	once	18	dieciocho	500	quinientos
5	cinco	12	doce	19	diecinueve	1,000	mil
6	seis	13	trece	20	veinte	10,000	diez mil

BASIC PHRASES

good morning	buenos días
good afternoon	buenas tardes
goodnight	buenas noches
goodbye	adiós
please	por favor
many thanks	muchas gracias
not at all	de nada
yes	sí
no	no
Pleased to meet you	Mucho gusto
How are you?	¿Cómo está usted?
Fine, thank you	Muy bien, gracias
Do you speak English?	¿Habla usted inglés?
I don't speak Spanish	No hablo español
I don't understand	No entiendo
What is your name?	¿Cuál es su nombre?
My name is...	Yo me llamo...
Where is (the)...?	¿Dónde está (el/la)...?
How much is...?	¿Cuánto es...?
What time is it?	¿Qué hora es?

DIRECTION

How can I get to...?	¿Cómo puedo llegar a...?
turn right	a la derecha
turn left	a la izquierda
straight on	derecho

TRANSPORT

bus	el autobus
train	el tren
car	el auto
petrol	la gasolina
parking	estacionamiento
it doesn't work	no funciona

PLACES

embassy	la embajada
hospital	el hospital/la clínica
toilet	el baño
post office	la casa de correos
chemist	la farmacia
tourist office	la oficina de turismo
petrol station	la gasolinera
doctor	el médico

FOOD

first course	entremeses
bread	pan
meat	carne
fish	pescado
pork	cerdo
chicken	pollo
lamb	cordero
veal	ternera
prawns	gambas
shrimp	camarones
salad	ensalada
dressing (oil/garlic)	al mojo de ajo
vegetables	vegetales
ice cream	helado
fruit	fruta
cream	crema

DRINKS

wine	vino
red, white, rosé	tinto, blanco, rosado
beer	cerveza
mineral water/ sparkling	agua mineral/ con gas
coffee	café
tea	te

OTHERS

breakfast	el desayuno
lunch	la comida
dinner	la cena
the bill, please	la cuenta, por favor

Mexico has a number of private and state-owned television channels. Cable and satellite TV companies provide hundreds of additional channels, many in English and other foreign languages.

The journalist and political analyst Ana Maria Salazar hosts a radio programme in English on weekdays at 5.30am and 11pm on FM 90.5 in Mexico City.

Money matters

Coins are in denominations of 10, 20 and 50 centavos, and 1, 2, 5, 10 and 20 pesos. Notes are in denominations of 20, 50, 100, 200 and 500 pesos. US dollars are often accepted in Mexico, and prices can sometimes be given in dollars.

All the major banks or their representatives are found in Mexico City and other main towns. If you have some identification, you can change traveller's cheques in most of the big banks and obtain cash against the major credit cards. Major credit cards that are widely accepted are American Express, Visa, MasterCard, Carte Blanche and Diners.

Traveller's cheques must be in US dollars. Thomas Cook MasterCard traveller's cheques free you from the hazards of carrying large amounts of cash, and in the event of loss or theft can quickly be refunded. Many hotels, restaurants and some shops in main tourist areas accept traveller's cheques.

National holidays

Dates marked with an asterisk (*) are not official holidays, but people generally don't work on these days.

1 January New Year's Day
6 January Epiphany*
5 February Constitution Day
21 March Benito Juárez Day
March/April Maundy Thursday/ Good Friday*
1 May Labour Day
5 May Battle of Puebla
1 September President's Report
16 September Independence Day
12 October Columbus Day (Day of the Race)
1 November All Saints' Day*
2 November Day of the Dead*
20 November Revolution Day
12 December Virgin of Guadalupe*
25 December Christmas Day

Opening hours

The following is a general guide only.
Banks Mon–Fri 9am–4pm (Sat 10am–1.30pm in certain cases).
Stores Mon–Sat 9am–8pm, or later in resorts. Many shops in the capital do not open until 11am.
Post offices Mon–Fri 8am–6pm.
Municipal and government buildings daily 8am–8pm.
Museums Tue–Sun 10am–5pm.
Churches and cathedrals daily 8am–1pm, 4–6pm.
Archaeological sites daily 8am–5pm.

Police

Tourist police, who wear square badges of red, green and white, are around in Mexico City. Some speak English, and you will find them friendly and willing.

Post offices

Most towns have a post office, with *poste restante* available (identification must be shown when collecting mail). Postboxes (*buzones*) are red.

Public transport

Air

Mexico has an extensive network of domestic air services linking all major towns and resorts. Air travel is a popular means of transport in Mexico, and flights are often full, so make advance reservations.

Bus and rail

Bus services range from luxury express buses with toilet and air-conditioning to the more basic short-distance buses. All towns have one or more bus terminals. Left-luggage facilities are available at the larger terminals.

Trains are even cheaper than buses, but are slow and unreliable. Highly recommended, however, is the Copper Canyon journey (*see pp140–41*).

Local transport

Mexico City's metro is efficient and incredibly cheap, but not recommended during peak hours. Local buses are packed and used mainly by locals. There are usually plenty of the metered green Volkswagen taxis about, but it's best to avoid these. The larger *sitios,* which take radio calls and also park outside hotels, charge a fixed price for the journey; this should be determined beforehand.

In the regions, taxis are generally plentiful. They have no meters and the fares are fixed, but normally inexpensive.

Student and youth travel

Students can get cheaper international flights through the Student Travel Centre in London (*tel: (020) 7434 1306*) or other student travel organisations. An International Student Identity Card (ISIC) can often get discounts on transport, museum entry, etc. (*For* Youth Hostels, *see p175.*)

Sustainable tourism

Thomas Cook is a strong advocate of ethical and fairly traded tourism and believes that the travel experience

Buena Vista railway station, Mexico City

should be as good for the places visited as it is for the people who visit them. That's why we firmly support The Travel Foundation, a charity that develops solutions to help improve and protect holiday destinations, their environment, traditions and culture. To find out what you can do to make a positive difference to the places you travel to and the people who live there, please visit

www.thetravelfoundation.org.uk

Telephones

Long-distance calls can be costly from your hotel, so try public booths (using a Ladatel card). Useful numbers are *090* (international operator); *040* (directory enquiries).

Time

Most of Mexico is on Central Standard Time (GMT minus 6 hours). The northwestern states operate on Mountain Time (GMT minus 7 hours). Baja California Norte is on Pacific Standard Time (GMT minus 8 hours).

Tipping

Service charges are rarely included in restaurants, and clients are expected to pay a 10–15 per cent tip. The exception is taxis: tips are not normally expected, unless the driver has been particularly helpful in some way.

Toilets

In major airports and good restaurants toilets are usually reasonable. In rural areas they can be discouraging. It helps to carry your own soap and toilet paper.

Tourist offices

The Secretaría de Turismo (Sectur) is the official Mexican Government Ministry of Tourism. The head office in Mexico City is located at Presidente Mazaryk 172, Polanco, with a 24-hour multilingual hotline information service (*tel: (55) 5250 0123*). Otherwise, *tel: (55) 3002 6300*.

All main towns and resorts have one or more tourist offices, with a list usually obtainable from your local Mexican tourist office.

Websites

www.visitmexico.com
Website for the Mexico Tourism Board.
www.go2mexico.com
ww.mexonline.com
www.knowmexico.com
www.mexperience.com
Good sources of travel tips, information and articles about Mexico.
www.gob.mx
Official Mexico Government website, in Spanish only.

Travellers with disabilities

Though Mexico is not by and large equipped for disabled travellers, wheelchairs are available at Mexico City airport and others on request. Certain hotels have at least one room or unit accessible to wheelchair users, and some inbound tour operators can provide them on tour.

Index

Acknowledgements

Thomas Cook wishes to thank the photographers, picture libraries and other organisations for the loan of the photographs reproduced in this book, to whom copyright in the photographs belongs.

FLICKR/Buggs 93, Escraper 77, Erlin1 151, Jungle Boy 151; FOTOLIA/Attilio G Peschiera 31, Terence Lee 65, Carlos Sanchez Pereyra 121, 145, Melva Vivian 127; ROBERT HARDING 149; PBASE/Elias Viguer 35; PICTURES COLOUR LIBRARY 28, 157, 164, 167, 170; SOUTH AMERICAN PICTURES/Chris Sharp 4, 9a, 23, 25, 61, 67, 95, 100, 101a, 122, 128, 129, 130, 142 148, 161, 171, 176, Tony Morisson 7, 47, 124, 125, 141b, 151a, Frank Nowikowski 24, 153, Robert Francis 18, 26, 28a, 85, 141a, Iain Pearson 101b, 155, 157, Rebecca Whitfield 48; WIKIMEDIA COMMONS/Agencia Brasil 13; WORLD PICTURES/PHOTOSHOOT 1, 17, 29, 39, 45, 50, 69, 76, 81, 87, 97, 102, 113, 163, 168, 182 185.

The remaining pictures are held in the AA PHOTO LIBRARY and were taken by: RICK STRANGE 9b, 14, 19, 21, 27, 33, 37, 38, 41, 45, 46, 52, 53, 59, 63, 69, 70, 71, 72, 73, 75, 79, 80, 82, 83, 84, 89, 103, 105, 106a, 106b, 107a, 107b, 108, 109, 110, 112, 133, 135a, 136, 138a, 138b, 139a, 139b, 143a, 143b, 144, 147, 151b, 159, 165, 167, 168, 173, 174, 179, 187; PETER WILSON 117, 118, 177; ERIC MEACHER 119.

PROOFREADER: IAN FAULKNER for CAMBRIDGE PUBLISHING MANAGEMENT LTD

SEND YOUR THOUGHTS TO BOOKS@THOMASCOOK.COM

We're committed to providing the very best up-to-date information in our travel guides and constantly strive to make them as useful as they can be. You can help us to improve future editions by letting us have your feedback. If you've made a wonderful discovery on your travels that we don't already feature, if you'd like to inform us about recent changes to anything that we do include, or if you simply want to let us know your thoughts about this guidebook and how we can make it even better – we'd love to hear from you.

Send us ideas, discoveries and recommendations today and then look out for your valuable input in the next edition of this title. And, as an extra 'thank you' from Thomas Cook Publishing, you'll be automatically entered into our exciting prize draw.

Emails to the above address, or letters to Travellers Project Editor, Thomas Cook Publishing, PO Box 227, Coningsby Road, Peterborough PE3 8SB, UK.

Please don't forget to let us know which title your feedback refers to!